FROM THE MAKER OF THE TEST

The Official SAT Subject Test Study Guide

Physics

The College Board
New York, N.Y.

About the College Board

The College Board is a mission-driven not-for-profit organization that connects students to college success and opportunity. Founded in 1900, the College Board was created to expand access to higher education. Today, the membership association is made up of over 6,000 of the world's leading educational institutions and is dedicated to promoting excellence and equity in education. Each year, the College Board helps more than seven million students prepare for a successful transition to college through programs and services in college readiness and college success—including the SAT® and the Advanced Placement Program®. The organization also serves the education community through research and advocacy on behalf of students, educators, and schools.

For further information, visit collegeboard.org.

Copies of this book are available from your bookseller or may be ordered from College Board Publications at store.collegeboard.org or by calling 800-323-7155.

Editorial inquiries concerning this book should be addressed to the College Board, SAT Program, 250 Vesey Street, New York, New York 10281.

ISBN 13: 978-1457309212

Printed in the United States of America

2 3 4 5 6 7 8 9   23 22 21 20 19 18

Distributed by Macmillan

Contents

The SAT Subject Tests™

About SAT Subject Tests

SAT Subject Tests™ are a valuable way to help you show colleges a more complete picture of your academic background and interests. Each year, nearly one million Subject Tests are taken by students throughout the country and around the world to gain admission to the leading colleges and universities in the U.S.

SAT Subject Tests are one-hour exams that give you the opportunity to demonstrate knowledge and showcase achievement in specific subjects. They provide a fair and reliable measure of your achievement in high school—information that can help enhance your college admission portfolio. The Physics Subject Test is a great way to highlight your understanding, skills, and strengths in physics.

This book provides information and guidance to help you study for and familiarize yourself with the Physics Subject Test. It contains actual, previously administered tests and official answer sheets that will help you get comfortable with the tests' format, so you feel better prepared on test day.

The Benefits of SAT Subject Tests

SAT Subject Tests let you put your best foot forward, allowing you to focus on subjects that you know well and enjoy. They can help you differentiate yourself in a competitive admission environment by providing additional information about your skills and knowledge of particular subjects. Many colleges also use Subject Tests for course placement and selection; some schools allow you to place out of introductory courses by taking certain Subject Tests.

Subject Tests are flexible and can be tailored to your strengths and areas of interest. These are the **only** national admission tests where **you** choose the tests that best showcase your achievements and interests. You select the Subject Test(s) and can take up to three tests in one sitting. With the exception of listening tests, you can even decide to change the subject or number of tests you want to take on the day of the test. This flexibility can help you be more relaxed on test day.

Who Should Consider Subject Tests?

Anyone can take an SAT Subject Test to highlight their knowledge of a specific subject. SAT Subject Tests may be especially beneficial for certain students:

- Students applying to colleges that require or recommend Subject Tests—be aware that some schools have additional Subject Test requirements for certain students, majors, or programs of study

- Students who wish to demonstrate strength in specific subject areas

- Students who wish to demonstrate knowledge obtained outside a traditional classroom environment (e.g., summer enrichment, distance learning, weekend study, etc.)

- Students looking to place out of certain classes in college

- Students enrolled in dual-enrollment programs

- Homeschooled students or students taking courses online

- Students who feel that their course grade may not be a true reflection of their knowledge of the subject matter

The SAT Subject Test in Physics is particularly useful for students interested in majors with a focus in STEM (Science, Technology, Engineering, and Math).

Who Requires the SAT Subject Tests?

Most college websites and catalogs include information about admission requirements, including which Subject Tests are needed or recommended for admission. Schools have varying policies regarding Subject Tests, but they generally fall into one or more of the following categories:

- Required for admission

- Recommended for admission

- Required or recommended for certain majors or programs of study (e.g., engineering, honors, etc.)

- Required or recommended for certain groups of students (e.g., homeschooled students)

- Required, recommended, or accepted for course placement

- Accepted for course credit

- Accepted as an alternative to fulfill certain college admission requirements

- Accepted as an alternative to fulfill certain high school subject competencies

- Accepted and considered, especially if Subject Tests improve or enhance a student's application

REMEMBER

Subject Tests are a valuable way to help you show colleges a more complete picture of your academic achievements.

In addition, the College Board provides a number of resources where you can search for information about Subject Test requirements at specific colleges.

- Visit the websites of the colleges and universities that interest you.
- Visit College Search at collegeboard.org.
- Purchase a copy of *The College Board College Handbook*.

Some colleges require specific tests, such as mathematics or science, so it's important to make sure you understand the policies prior to choosing which Subject Test(s) to take. If you have questions or concerns about admission policies, contact college admission officers at individual schools. They are usually pleased to meet with students interested in their schools.

Subject Tests Offered

SAT Subject Tests measure how well you know a particular subject area and your ability to apply that knowledge. SAT Subject Tests aren't connected to specific textbooks or teaching methods. The content of each test evolves to reflect the latest trends in what is taught in typical high school courses in the corresponding subject.

The tests fall into five general subject areas:

English	History	Mathematics	Science	Languages	
				Reading Only	**with Listening**
Literature	United States History	Mathematics Level 1	Biology E/M	French	Chinese
	World History	Mathematics Level 2	Chemistry	German	French
			Physics	Italian	German
				Latin	Japanese
				Modern Hebrew	Korean
				Spanish	Spanish

Who Develops the Tests

The SAT Subject Tests are part of the SAT® Program of the College Board, a not-for-profit membership association of over 6,000 schools, colleges, universities, and other educational associations. Every year, the College Board serves seven million students and their parents; 24,000 high schools; and 3,800 colleges through major programs and services in college readiness, college admission, guidance, assessment, financial aid, and enrollment.

Each subject has its own test development committee, typically composed of teachers and college professors appointed for the different Subject Tests. The test questions are written and reviewed by each Subject Test Committee, under the guidance of professional test developers. The tests are rigorously developed, highly reliable assessments of knowledge and skills taught in high school classrooms.

Deciding to Take an SAT Subject Test

Which Tests Should You Take?

The SAT Subject Test(s) that you take should be based on your interests and academic strengths. The tests are a great way to indicate interest in specific majors or programs of study (e.g., engineering, pre-med, cultural studies).

You should also consider whether the colleges that you're interested in require or recommend Subject Tests. Some colleges will grant an exemption from or credit for a freshman course requirement if a student does well on a particular SAT Subject Test. Below are some things for you to consider as you decide which test(s) to take.

Think through your strengths and interests

- List the subjects in which you do well and that truly interest you.

- Think through what you might like to study in college.

- Consider whether your current admission credentials (high school grades, SAT scores, etc.) highlight your strengths.

Consider the colleges that you're interested in

- Make a list of the colleges you're considering.

- Take some time to look into what these colleges require or what may help you stand out in the admission process.

- Use College Search to look up colleges' test requirements.

- If the colleges you're interested in require or recommend SAT Subject Tests, find out how many tests are required or recommended and in which subjects.

Take a look at your current and recent course load

- Have you completed the required coursework? The best time to take SAT Subject Tests is at the end of the course, when the material is still fresh in your mind.

- Check the recommended preparation guidelines for the Subject Tests that interest you to see if you've completed the recommended coursework.

- Try your hand at some SAT Subject Test practice questions on collegeboard.org or in this book.

Don't forget, regardless of admission requirements, you can enhance your college portfolio by taking Subject Tests in subject areas that you know very well.

If you're still unsure about which SAT Subject Test(s) to take, talk to your teacher or counselor about your specific situation. You can also find more information about SAT Subject Tests on collegeboard.org.

When to Take the Tests

We generally recommend that you take the Physics Subject Test after you complete physics course(s), prior to your senior year of high school, if possible. This way, you will already have your Subject Test credentials complete, allowing you to focus on your college applications in the fall of your senior year. Try to take the test soon after your courses end, when the content is still fresh in your mind.

Since not all Subject Tests are offered on every test date, be sure to check when the Subject Tests that you're interested in are offered and plan accordingly.

You should also balance this with college application deadlines. If you're interested in applying early decision or early action to any college, many colleges advise that you take the SAT Subject Tests by October or November of your senior year. For regular decision applications, some colleges will accept SAT Subject Test scores through the December administration. Use College Search to look up policies for specific colleges.

This book suggests ways you can prepare for the Subject Tests in Physics. Before taking a test in a subject you haven't studied recently, ask your teacher for advice about the best time to take the test. Then review the course material thoroughly over several weeks.

How to Register for the Tests

There are several ways to register for the SAT Subject Tests.

- Visit the College Board's website at collegeboard.org. Most students choose to register for Subject Tests on the College Board website.

- Register by telephone (for a fee) if you have registered previously for the SAT or an SAT Subject Test. Call, toll free from anywhere in the United States, 866-756-7346. From outside the United States, call 212-713-7789.

- If you do not have access to the internet, find registration forms in *The Paper Registration Guide for the SAT and SAT Subject Tests*. You can find the booklet in a guidance office at any high school or by writing to:

  The College Board
  SAT Program
  P.O. Box 025505
  Miami, FL 33102

When you register for the SAT Subject Tests, you will have to indicate the specific Subject Tests you plan to take on the test date you select. You may take one, two, or three tests on any given test date; your testing fee will vary accordingly. Except for the Language Tests with Listening, you may change your mind on the day of the test and instead select from any of the other Subject Tests offered that day.

Student Search Service

The Student Search Service helps colleges find prospective students. If you take the PSAT/NMSQT®, the SAT, an SAT Subject Test, or any AP® Exam, you can be included in this free service.

Here's how it works: During SAT or SAT Subject Test registration, indicate that you want to be part of the Student Search. Your name is put in a database along with other information such as your address, high school grade point average, date of birth, grade level, high school, email address, intended college major, and extracurricular activities.

Colleges and scholarship programs then use the Student Search to help them locate and recruit students with characteristics that might be a good match with their schools.

Here are some points to keep in mind about the Student Search Service:

- Being part of Student Search is voluntary. You may take the test even if you don't join Student Search.

- Colleges participating in Student Search do not receive your exam scores. Colleges can ask for the names of students within certain score ranges, but your exact score is not reported.

- Being contacted by a college doesn't mean you have been admitted. You can be admitted only after you apply. The Student Search Service is simply a way for colleges to reach prospective students.

- Student Search Service will share your contact information only with approved colleges and scholarship programs that are recruiting students like you. Your name will never be sold to a private company or mailing list.

Keep the Tests in Perspective

Colleges that require Subject Test scores do so because the scores are useful in making admission or placement decisions. Schools that don't have specific Subject Test policies generally review them during the application process because the scores can give a fuller picture of your academic achievement. The Subject Tests are a particularly helpful tool for admission and placement programs because the tests aren't tied to specific textbooks, grading procedures, or instruction methods but are still tied to curricula. The tests provide level ground on which colleges can compare your scores with those of students who come from schools and backgrounds that may be far different from yours.

It's important to remember that test scores are just one of several factors that colleges consider in the admission process. Admission officers also look at your high school grades, letters of recommendation, extracurricular activities, essays, and other criteria. Try to keep this in mind when you're preparing for and taking Subject Tests.

Fee Waivers

Students who face financial barriers to taking the SAT Subject Tests can be granted College Board fee waivers through schools and authorized community-based organizations to cover the cost of testing. Seniors who use a fee waiver to take the SAT will automatically receive four college application fee waivers to use in applying to colleges and universities that accept the waivers. You can learn about eligibility and other benefits offered to help you in the college application process at sat.org/fee-waivers.

Score Choice

In March 2009, the College Board introduced Score Choice, a feature that gives you the option to choose the scores you send to colleges by test date for the SAT and by individual test for the SAT Subject Tests—at no additional cost. Designed to reduce your test day stress, Score Choice gives you an opportunity to show colleges the scores you feel best represent your abilities. Score Choice is optional, so if you don't actively choose to use it, all of your scores will be sent automatically with your score report. Because most colleges only consider your best scores, you should still feel comfortable reporting scores from all of your tests.

REMEMBER
Score Choice gives you an opportunity to show colleges the scores you feel best represent your abilities.

About collegeboard.org

The College Board website collegeboard.org is a comprehensive tool that can help you be prepared, connected, and informed throughout the college planning and admission process. In addition to registering for the SAT and SAT Subject Tests, you can find information about other tests and services, browse the College Board Store (where you can order *The Official Study Guide for All SAT Subject Tests* and other guides specific to mathematics and sciences), and send emails with your questions and concerns. You can also find free practice questions for each of the 20 SAT Subject Tests. These are an excellent supplement to this Study Guide and can help you be even more prepared on test day.

Once you create a free online account, you can print your SAT admission ticket, see your scores, and send them to schools.

More college planning resources The College Board offers free, comprehensive resources at Big Future™ to help you with your college planning. Visit **bigfuture.org** to put together a step-by-step plan for the entire process, from finding the right college, exploring majors and careers, and calculating costs, to applying for scholarships and financial aid.

How to Do Your Best on the SAT Subject Test

Get Ready

Give yourself plenty of time to review the material in this book before test day. The rules for the SAT Subject Tests may be different than the rules for most of the tests you've taken in high school. You're probably used to answering questions in order, spending more time answering the hard questions, and, in the hopes of getting at least partial credit, showing all your work.

When you take the SAT Subject Tests, it's OK to move around within the test section and to answer questions in any order you wish. Keep in mind that the questions go from easier to harder. You receive one point for each question answered correctly. No partial credit is given, and only those answers entered on the answer sheet are scored. For each question that you try but answer incorrectly, a fraction of a point is subtracted from the total number of correct answers. No points are added or subtracted for unanswered questions. If your final raw score includes a fraction, the score is rounded to the nearest whole number.

Avoid Surprises

Know what to expect. Become familiar with the test and test day procedures. You'll boost your confidence and feel a lot more relaxed.

- **Know how the tests are set up.** All SAT Subject Tests are one-hour multiple-choice tests. The first page of each Subject Test includes a background questionnaire. You will be asked to fill it out before taking the test. The information is for statistical purposes only. It will not influence your test score. Your answers to the questionnaire will assist us in developing future versions of the test. You can see a sample of the background questionnaire for the Physics Subject Test at the start of each practice test in this book.

- **Learn the test directions.** The directions for answering the questions in this book are the same as those on the actual test. If you become familiar with the directions now, you'll leave yourself more time to answer the questions when you take the test.

- **Study the sample questions.** The more familiar you are with question formats, the more comfortable you'll feel when you see similar questions on the actual test.

- **Get to know the answer sheet.** At the back of this book, you'll find a set of sample answer sheets. The appearance of the answer sheets in this book may differ from the answer sheets you see on test day.

- **Understand how the tests are scored.** You get one point for each right answer and lose a fraction of a point for each wrong answer. You neither gain nor lose points for omitting an answer. Hard questions count the same amount as easier questions.

A Practice Test Can Help

Find out where your strengths lie and which areas you need to work on. Do a run-through of a Subject Test under conditions that are close to what they will be on test day.

- **Set aside an hour so you can take the test without interruption.** You will be given one hour to take each SAT Subject Test.

- **Prepare a desk or table that has no books or papers on it.** No books, including dictionaries, are allowed in the test room.

- **Read the instructions that precede the practice test.** On test day, you will be asked to do this before you answer the questions.

- **Remove and fill in an answer sheet from the back of this book.** You can use one answer sheet for up to three Subject Tests.

- **Use a clock or kitchen timer to time yourself.** This will help you to pace yourself and to get used to taking a test in 60 minutes.

The Day Before the Test

It's natural to be nervous. A bit of a nervous edge can keep you sharp and focused. Below are a few suggestions to help you be more relaxed as the test approaches.

Do a brief review on the day before the test. Look through the sample questions, answer explanations, and test directions in this book or on the College Board website. Keep the review brief; cramming the night before the test is unlikely to help your performance and might even make you more anxious.

The night before test day, prepare everything you need to take with you. You will need:

- Your admission ticket.
- An acceptable photo ID (see page 11).
- Two No. 2 pencils with soft erasers. Do not bring pens or mechanical pencils.
- A watch without an audible alarm.
- A snack.

Know the route to the test center and any instructions for finding the entrance.

Check the time your admission ticket specifies for arrival. Arrive a little early to give yourself time to settle in.

Get a good night's sleep.

Acceptable Photo IDs

- Driver's license (with your photo)
- State-issued ID
- Valid passport
- School ID card
- Student ID form that has been prepared by your school on school stationery and includes a recognizable photo and the school seal, which overlaps the photo (go to collegeboard.org for more information)

The most up-to-date information about acceptable photo IDs can be found on collegeboard.org.

REMINDER   **What I Need on Test Day**

Make a copy of this box and post it somewhere noticeable.

I Need   **I Have**

Appropriate photo ID

Admission ticket

Two No. 2 pencils with clean soft erasers

Watch (without an audible alarm)

Snack

Bottled water

Directions to the test center

Instructions for finding the entrance on weekends

I am leaving the house at _____ a.m.

Be on time or you can't take the test.

On Test Day

You have a good reason to feel confident. You're thoroughly prepared. You're familiar with what this day will bring. You are in control.

Keep in Mind

You must be on time or you can't take the test. Leave yourself plenty of time for mishaps and emergencies.

Think positively. If you are worrying about not doing well, then your mind isn't on the test. Be as positive as possible.

Stay focused. Think only about the question in front of you. Letting your mind wander will cost you time.

Concentrate on your own test. The first thing some students do when they get stuck on a question is to look around to see how everyone else is doing. What they usually see is that others seem busy filling in their answer sheets. Instead of being concerned that you are not doing as well as everyone else, keep in mind that everyone works at a different pace. Your neighbors may not be working on the question that puzzled you. They may not even be taking the same test. Thinking about what others are doing takes you away from working on your own test.

Making an Educated Guess

Educated guesses are helpful when it comes to taking tests with multiple-choice questions; however, making random guesses is not a good idea. To correct for random guessing, a fraction of a point is subtracted for each incorrect answer. That means random guessing—guessing with no idea of an answer that might be correct—could lower your score. The best approach is to eliminate all the choices that you know are wrong. Make an educated guess from the remaining choices. If you can't eliminate any choice, move on.

REMEMBER

All correct answers are worth one point, regardless of the question's difficulty level.

IMPORTANT

Cell phones are not allowed to be used in the test center or the testing room. If your cell phone is on, your scores will be canceled.

10 Tips FOR TAKING THE TEST

1. **Read carefully.** Consider all the choices in each question. Avoid careless mistakes that will cause you to lose points.

2. **Answer the easier questions first.** Work on less time-consuming questions before moving on to the more difficult ones.

3. **Eliminate choices that you know are wrong.** Cross them out in your test book so that you can clearly see which choices are left.

4. **Make educated guesses or skip the question.** If you have eliminated the choices that you know are wrong, guessing is your best strategy. However, if you cannot eliminate any of the answer choices, it is best to skip the question.

5. **Keep your answer sheet neat.** The answer sheet is scored by a machine, which can't tell the difference between an answer and a doodle. If the machine mistakenly reads two answers for one question, it will consider the question unanswered.

6. **Use your test booklet as scrap paper.** Use it to make notes or write down ideas. No one else will look at what you write.

7. **Check off questions as you work on them.** This will save time and help you to know which questions you've skipped.

8. **Check your answer sheet regularly.** Make sure you are in the right place. Check the number of the question and the number on the answer sheet every few questions. This is especially important when you skip a question. Losing your place on the answer sheet will cost you time and may cost you points.

9. **Work at an even, steady pace and keep moving.** Each question on the test takes a certain amount of time to read and answer. Good test-takers develop a sense of timing to help them complete the test. Your goal is to spend time on the questions that you are most likely to answer correctly.

10. **Keep track of time.** During the hour that each Subject Test takes, check your progress occasionally so that you know how much of the test you have completed and how much time is left. Leave a few minutes for review toward the end of the testing period.

IMPORTANT

If you erase all your answers to a Subject Test, that's the same as a request to cancel the test. All Subject Tests taken with the erased test will also be canceled.

REMEMBER

Check your answer sheet. Make sure your answers are dark and completely filled in. Erase completely.

7 Ways TO PACE YOURSELF

1. Set up a schedule. Know when you should be one-quarter of the way through and halfway through. Every now and then, check your progress against your schedule.

2. Begin to work as soon as the testing time begins. Reading the instructions and getting to know the test directions in this book ahead of time will allow you to do that.

3. Work at an even, steady pace. After you answer the questions you are sure of, move on to those for which you'll need more time.

4. Skip questions you can't answer. You might have time to return to them. Remember to mark them in your test booklet, so you'll be able to find them later.

5. As you work on a question, cross out the answers you can eliminate in your test book.

6. Go back to the questions you skipped. If you can, eliminate some of the answer choices, then make an educated guess.

7. Leave time in the last few minutes to check your answers to avoid mistakes.

After the Tests

Most, but not all, scores will be reported online several weeks after the test date. A few days later, a full score report will be available to you online. Your score report will also be mailed to your high school and to the colleges, universities, and scholarship programs that you indicated on your registration form or on the correction form attached to your admission ticket. The score report includes your scores, percentiles, and interpretive information. You will only receive a paper score report if you indicate that you would like one.

What's Your Score?

Scores are available for free at collegeboard.org several weeks after each SAT is given. You can also get your scores—for a fee—by telephone. Call Customer Service at (866) 756-7346 in the United States. From outside the United States, dial (212) 713-7789.

Some scores may take longer to report. If your score report is not available online when expected, check back the following week. If you have not received your mailed score report by eight weeks after the test date (by five weeks for online reports), contact Customer Service by phone at (866) 756-7346 or by email at sat@info.collegeboard.org.

Should You Take the Tests Again?

Before you decide whether or not to retest, you need to evaluate your scores. The best way to evaluate how you really did on a Subject Test is to compare your scores to the admissions or placement requirements, or average scores, of the colleges to which you are applying. You may decide that with additional work you could do better taking the test again.

? Contacting the College Board

If you have comments or questions about the tests, please write to us at the College Board SAT Program, P.O. Box 025505, Miami, FL 33102, or email us at sat@info.collegeboard.org.

Physics

Purpose

The Subject Test in Physics measures the knowledge you would be expected to have after successfully completing a college preparatory course in high school. The test is not based on any one textbook or instructional approach but concentrates on the common core of material found in most texts.

Format

This one-hour test consists of 75 multiple-choice questions. Topics that are covered in most high school courses are emphasized. Because high school courses differ, both in percentage of time devoted to each major topic and in the specific subtopics covered, most students will find that there are some questions on topics with which they are not familiar.

Content

This test covers topics listed in the chart on the next page.

Topics Covered

Topics	Approximate Percentage of Test
I. Mechanics	36–42%

Kinematics, such as velocity, acceleration, motion in one dimension, motion of projectiles

Dynamics, such as force, Newton's laws, statics, friction

Energy and Momentum, such as potential and kinetic energy, work, power, impulse, conservation laws

Circular Motion, such as uniform circular motion and centripetal force

Simple Harmonic Motion, such as mass on a spring and the pendulum

Gravity, such as the law of gravitation, orbits, Kepler's Laws

Topics	Approximate Percentage of Test
II. Electricity and Magnetism	18–24%

Electric Fields, Forces, and Potentials, such as Coulomb's law, induced charge, field and potential of groups of point charges, charged particles in electric fields

Capacitance, such as parallel-plate capacitors and transients

Circuit Elements and DC Circuits, such as resistors, light bulbs, series and parallel networks, Ohm's law, Joule's law

Magnetism, such as permanent magnets, fields caused by currents, particles in magnetic fields, Faraday's law, Lenz's law

Topics	Approximate Percentage of Test
III. Waves and Optics	15–19%

General Wave Properties, such as wave speed, frequency, wavelength, superposition, standing waves, Doppler effect

Reflection and Refraction, such as Snell's law, changes in wavelength and speed

Ray Optics, such as image formation using pinholes, mirrors, and lenses

Physical Optics, such as single-slit diffraction, double-slit interference, polarization, color

Topics	Approximate Percentage of Test
IV. Heat and Thermodynamics	6–11%

Thermal Properties, such as temperature, heat transfer, specific and latent heats, thermal expansion

Laws of Thermodynamics, such as first and second laws, internal energy, entropy, heat engine efficiency

Topics	Approximate Percentage of Test
V. Modern Physics	6–11%

Quantum Phenomena, such as photons, photoelectric effect

Atomic, such as the Rutherford and Bohr models, atomic energy levels, atomic spectra

Nuclear and Particle Physics, such as radioactivity, nuclear reactions, fundamental particles

Relativity, such as time dilation, length contraction, mass-energy equivalence

Topics	Approximate Percentage of Test
VI. Miscellaneous	4–9%

General, such as history of physics and general questions that overlap several major topics

Analytical Skills, such as graphical analysis, measurement, math skills

Contemporary Physics, such as astrophysics, superconductivity, chaos theory

How to Prepare

The test is intended for students who have completed a one-year introductory physics course at the college preparatory level. You should be able to

- recall and understand the major concepts of physics and to apply these physical principles you have learned to solve specific problems

- understand simple algebraic, trigonometric, and graphical relationships, and the concepts of ratio and proportion and apply these to physics problems

- apply laboratory skills in the context of physics

Laboratory experience is a significant factor in developing reasoning and problem-solving skills. This multiple-choice test can measure laboratory skills only in a limited way, such as data analysis. Familiarize yourself with directions in advance. The directions in this book are identical to those that appear on the test.

Skills Specification	Approximate Percentage of Test
Recall	20–33%
Generally involves remembering and understanding concepts or information	
Single-Concept Problem	40–53%
Recall and use of a single physical relationship	
Multiple-Concept Problem	20–33%
Recall and integration of two or more physical relationships	
Laboratory Skills	
In each of the six major content topics, some questions may deal with laboratory skills in context	

Notes: (1) This test assumes that the direction of any current is the direction of flow of positive charge (conventional current).

(2) Calculator use is not allowed during the test.

(3) Numerical calculations are not emphasized and are limited to simple arithmetic.

(4) This test predominantly uses the metric system.

Score

The total score for each test is reported on the 200 to 800 scale.

Sample Questions

Two types of questions are used in the Subject Test in Physics and are shown in the following samples. All questions in the test are multiple-choice questions in which you must choose the BEST response from the five choices offered.

Classification Questions

Each set of classification questions includes five lettered choices that you will use to answer all of the questions in the set. These choices appear before the questions in the set. In addition, there may be descriptive material that is relevant in answering the questions in the set. The choices may take various forms, such as words, phrases, sentences, graphs, pictures, equations, or data. The numbered questions themselves may also take such forms, or they may be given in the question format directly. To answer each question, select the lettered choice that provides the most appropriate response. You should consider all of the lettered choices before answering a question. The directions for this type of question state specifically that a choice cannot be eliminated just because it is the correct answer to a previous question.

Because the same five choices are applicable to several questions, the classification questions usually require less reading than other types of multiple-choice questions. Therefore, classification questions provide a quick means, in terms of testing time, of determining how well you have mastered the topics represented. The set of questions may ask you to recall appropriate information, or the set may ask you to apply information to a specific situation or to translate information between different forms (descriptive, graphical, mathematical). Thus, different types of abilities can be tested by this type of question.

Directions: Each set of lettered choices that follows refers to the numbered questions immediately following it. Select the one lettered choice that best answers each question and then fill in the corresponding circle on the answer sheet. A choice may be used once, more than once, or not at all in each set.

Questions 1–3 refer to the labeled arrows in the diagram below that shows two direct current electrical circuits.

The two circuits are both in the plane of the page with the battery configurations shown. The wire of circuit X passes between the poles of a permanent magnet. Arrow *A* points up out of the plane of the paper. Arrow *E* follows a circle that comes out of the paper on the left side of the wire and goes back into the paper on the right side of the wire.

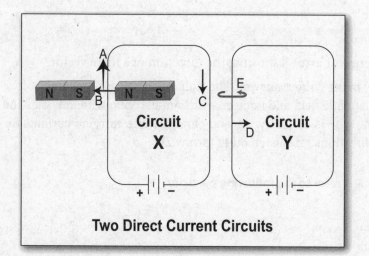

Two Direct Current Circuits

A) Arrow *A* only

B) Arrow *B* only

C) Arrow *C* only

D) Arrows *A* and *D*

E) Arrows *B* and *E*

1

The arrow or arrows showing the direction of conventional current flow.

Choice (C) is the correct answer. Conventional current flows from the positive terminal of the battery or power source to the negative terminal of the battery or power source. The other arrows show directions of force vectors and magnetic fields.

2

The arrow or arrows showing the direction of a magnetic field line.

Choice (E) is the correct answer. The magnetic field of a permanent magnet is directed from N to S (arrow *B*), and the right-hand rule shows the direction of magnetic field lines with respect to the direction of current flow (arrow *E*). The other arrows show force vectors and current direction.

3

The arrow or arrows showing the direction of a force vector.

Choice (D) is the correct answer. The right-hand rule for directions of current, magnetic field and force on a current-carrying wire indicates the force on the wire is up (arrow *A*), and parallel wires carrying currents in opposite directions repel each other (arrow *D*).

Questions 4–5 refer to the following particles.

A) Alpha
B) Electron
C) Neutron
D) Photon
E) Proton

4

Which particle could be put in place of the question mark to balance this equation? $^{238}_{92}\text{U} \rightarrow \,^{234}_{90}\text{Th} + ?$

Choice (A) is the correct answer. An alpha particle is a helium nucleus, which is written as $^{4}_{2}\text{He}$. The superscript 4 balances the number of nucleons (i.e., the atomic mass) and the subscript 2 balances the number of protons (i.e., the atomic number).

5

Which particle changes energy levels to create the absorption and emission spectra of atoms?

Choice (B) is the correct answer. The absorption and emission spectra are generated by the energy emitted when electrons are transferred from lower to higher or from higher to lower energy levels.

Five-Choice Completion Questions

The five-choice completion question is written either as an incomplete statement or as a question. In its simplest application, it poses a problem that intrinsically has a unique solution. It is also appropriate when (1) the problem presented is clearly delineated by the wording of the question so that you choose not a universal solution but the best of the five offered solutions; (2) the problem is such that you are required to evaluate the relevance of five plausible, or scientifically accurate, choices and to select the one most pertinent; or (3) the problem has several pertinent solutions and you are required to select the one that is *inappropriate* or *not correct* from among the five choices presented. Questions of this latter type will normally contain a word in capital letters such as NOT, EXCEPT, or LEAST.

A special type of five-choice completion question is used in some tests to allow for the possibility of more than one correct answer. Unlike many quantitative problems that must by their nature have one unique solution, situations do arise in which there may be more than one correct answer. In such situations, you should evaluate each answer independently of the others in order to select the most appropriate combination. In questions of this type, several (usually three) statements labeled by Roman numerals are given with the question. One or more of these statements may correctly answer the question. The statements are followed by five lettered choices, with each choice consisting of some combination of the Roman numerals that label the statements. You must select from among the five lettered choices the one that gives the combination of statements that best answers the question. In the test, questions of this type are intermixed among the more standard five-choice completion questions.

The five-choice completion question also tests problem-solving skills. With this type of question, you may be asked to convert the information given in a word problem into graphical forms or to select and apply the mathematical relationship necessary to solve the scientific problem. Alternatively, you may be asked to interpret experimental data, graphs, or mathematical expressions. Thus, the five-choice completion question can be adapted to test several kinds of abilities.

When the experimental data or other scientific problems to be analyzed are comparatively long, it is often convenient to organize several five-choice completion questions into sets, with each question in the set relating to the same common material that precedes the set. This practice allows you to answer several questions based on information that may otherwise take considerable testing time to read and comprehend. Such sets also test how thorough your understanding is of a particular situation. Although the questions in a set may be related, you do not have to know the answer to one question in a set to answer a subsequent question correctly. Each question in a set can be answered directly from the common material given for the entire set.

Directions: Each of the questions or incomplete statements that follows is followed by five suggested answers or completions. Select the one that is best in each case and then fill in the corresponding circle on the answer sheet.

6

Four identical objects are dropped or thrown from the top of a 10-meter high bridge at the same time. The objects are dropped or thrown as follows:

    I. Object 1 is dropped straight down with an initial speed of 0 m/s.

    II. Object 2 is thrown straight up with an initial speed of 5 m/s.

    III. Object 3 is thrown horizontally with an initial speed of 10 m/s.

    IV. Object 4 is thrown horizontally with an initial speed of 20 m/s.

Which objects will land in the water beneath the bridge at the same time? (Ignore the effect of air resistance.)

A) I and II only

B) II and III only

C) III and IV only

D) I, III and IV only

E) I, II, III and IV

Choice (D) is the correct answer. Object 2 will be delayed while it accelerates from an initial velocity of 5 m/s upward to a velocity of 0 m/s (at which point it will also have farther to fall). Only the downward force, the force of gravity, affects the downward acceleration for objects in free fall. Because objects 1, 3 and 4 have zero initial velocity in the vertical direction, they will land in the water beneath the bridge at the same time. Horizontal velocity is a separate vector from downward velocity. It does not increase "hang time" because the force of gravity downward is the same for all objects; all falling objects accelerate at the same rate. Therefore, objects 1, 3 and 4 will cover the distance to the water in the same amount of time.

7

A helicopter rises at constant speed to an altitude of h in time t. If the helicopter has mass m and the magnitude of acceleration due to gravity is g, what is the power needed for the helicopter to rise?

A) mgt

B) mgh

C) mgh/t

D) mgt/h^2

E) $\frac{1}{2}m(h/t)^2$

Choice (C) is the correct answer. Power is a measure of the rate at which work is done. The work done to raise the helicopter equals the change in energy of the helicopter. When increased to a height of h, the helicopter gains gravitational potential energy equal to mgh. The power needed for the helicopter to rise is then equal to the change in energy divided by the time. Mathematical expressions describing this problem are: $P = W/t = \Delta E/t = mgh/t$, where P is power, W is work, t is time, ΔE is change in energy, m is mass, g is acceleration due to gravity and h is height.

8

A player kicks a soccer ball from the ground with an initial velocity of 10 m/s. The ball leaves the ground at an angle of 23° above the horizontal field.

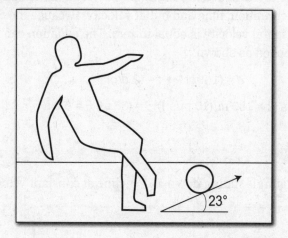

Given that sin 23° = 0.4, cos 23° = 0.9, and $g = 10$ m/s^2, approximately how far away does the ball land? (Ignore the effect of air resistance.)

A) 3.6 m

B) 4.0 m

C) 4.5 m

D) 7.2 m

E) 9.0 m

Choice (D) is the correct answer. The vertical velocity vector equals $v_y = v_0 \sin 23° = 10 \times 0.40 = 4$ m/s, and the ball reaches its maximum height at time = (4 m/s)/(10 m/s^2) = 0.4 seconds, so the ball travels for a total of 0.8 seconds. The horizontal velocity vector is $v_x = v_0 \cos 23° = 10 \times .9 = 9$ m/s. Therefore, the distance from where the ball was kicked to the point where the ball hits the ground is $d = v_x t = 9 \times 0.8 = 7.2$ m.

9

During a long climb, a rock climber stops to rest and eat an orange. She accidentally drops the orange and it falls to the ground 180 meters below. Assuming negligible air resistance and using 10 m/s² for the acceleration due to gravity, how long does it take the orange to reach the ground?

A) 3.0 s

B) 4.2 s

C) 6.0 s

D) 18 s

E) 36 s

Choice (C) is the correct answer. The time it takes for the orange to reach the ground can be calculated using the kinematic equation relating displacement, acceleration, time and initial velocity. Because the orange was dropped, its initial velocity is equal to zero. The equation can be simplified and applied as shown:

$$d = (1/2)gt^2 \rightarrow t = (2\ d/g)^{1/2}$$

$$t = (2 \times 180\ \text{m}/(10\ \text{m/s}^2))^{1/2} = (36\ \text{s}^2)^{1/2} = 6.0\ \text{s}$$

10

A 100 N penguin is sliding down a 7° incline at constant velocity.

What is the force of friction on the penguin? (sin 7° = 0.12)

A) 0.0012 N

B) 0.07 N

C) 12 N

D) 70 N

E) 100 N

Choice (C) is the correct answer. The component of the penguin's weight parallel to the surface of the incline equals 100 sin 7° = 12 N. Because velocity is constant, the forces acting on the penguin are balanced. Therefore the force of friction pointing up the incline is equal to the 12 N force pointing down the incline.

11

At time = 0, a 500 N skydiver jumps out of a stationary helicopter and accelerates until she reaches a constant velocity. One minute later, the skydiver opens a parachute and accelerates until she reaches a constant velocity again. If an upward force is positive, which two graphs together show the upward and downward forces on the skydiver over time?

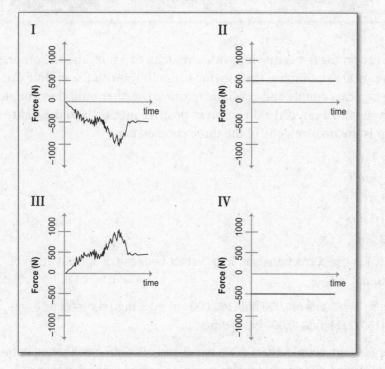

A) I and III

B) I and IV

C) II and III

D) II and IV

E) III and IV

Choice (E) is the correct answer. The graphs show unbalanced forces during acceleration and balanced forces when velocity is constant. The skydiver accelerates at first, when the upward force of air resistance is smaller than the downward force of gravity. The upward force increases until the forces are balanced and velocity becomes constant. When the parachute opens, the forces are unbalanced again because the upward force of air resistance becomes greater than the downward force of gravity. Then forces become balanced again when a new constant velocity is reached. Choice (A) is incorrect because it shows two forces that vary but are always balanced, which would indicate constant velocity. Choices (B) and (C) are incorrect because they show forces that cannot be balanced at any time; in choice (B) the forces are both negative, and in choice (C) the forces are both positive. Choice (D) is incorrect because it shows two forces that are both constant and always balanced, representing constant velocity the entire time.

12

Three railway cars, each with a mass of 80,000 kg, are on the same track.

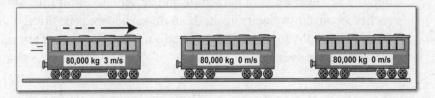

The car on the left is moving with a velocity of 3 m/s, and the other two cars are stationary. The moving car collides with the middle car. The two cars couple and continue to move together until they couple with the third car. If the direction of positive motion is to the right, what is the final velocity of the three coupled cars?

A) −3 m/s

B) −1 m/s

C) 1 m/s

D) 1.5 m/s

E) 3 m/s

Choice (C) is the correct answer. It is correct because of conservation of momentum:

$m_1 v_1 = m_2 v_2$; $v_2 = 3$ m/s (80,000 kg)/(160,000 kg) = 1.5 m/s. $m_2 v_2 = m_3 v_3$; $v_3 =$ 1.5 m/s (160,000 kg)/(240,000 kg) = 1 m/s

Because the cars couple, there is no recoil and all motion continues in the positive direction. The problem also could be solved with: $m_1 v_1 = m_3 v_3$.

Conceptually, if the mass triples, then the velocity will decrease by a factor of 3. Choice (A) is incorrect because only the mass of one car was used, and because the sign is wrong. Choice (B) is incorrect because the sign is wrong; there is no reversal of direction because there is no recoil. Choice (D) is incorrect because the mass of two, not three, cars was used. Choice (E) is incorrect because the mass of only one car was used.

13

An airbag reduces injury to a passenger during a car crash. This benefit is due primarily to which of the following?

A) The air bag reduces the force by reducing the passenger's change in velocity.

B) The air bag reduces the change in momentum by increasing the passenger's impulse.

C) The air bag reduces the impulse by reducing the change in the passenger's momentum.

D) The air bag reduces the force by increasing the time it takes the passenger to stop moving.

E) The air bag reduces the change in velocity by reducing the time it takes the passenger to stop moving.

Choice (D) is the correct answer. Impulse equals force times the time over which it acts. Impulse also equals mass times change in velocity—that is, change in momentum: $F\Delta t = m\Delta v$

Velocity must go to zero, so Δv is constant. The mass (m) of the passenger is also constant. However, both the force (F) and the time it takes the passenger to stop moving (Δt) can change as long as the product ($F\Delta t$) is constant. Presumably, the air bag applies a force over a longer period of time than would the dashboard or windshield. The increase in contact time results in a decrease in force applied to the passenger. Choices (A) and (E) are incorrect because the change in velocity (Δv) is constant. Choices (B) and (C) are incorrect because impulse ($m\Delta v$) does not change, as both the change in velocity and mass are constant. Choices (A) and (E) are incorrect because the change in velocity (Δv) is constant.

14

A disk with a 0.20 meter diameter is spinning once per second. What is the centripetal acceleration of a point on the edge of this disk?

A) 0.04π m/s^2

B) 0.20π m/s^2

C) $0.16\pi^2$ m/s^2

D) $0.40\pi^2$ m/s^2

E) $0.80\pi^2$ m/s^2

Choice (D) is the correct answer. $a_c = 4\pi^2 r/T^2$

The radius r is half the diameter, or 0.1 m, and the period T is 1.0 s. Then, $a_c = 4\pi^2(0.1)/(1.0)^2 = 0.40\pi^2$m/s^2.

Choice (A) is incorrect because it uses a different formula, $4\pi r^2$. This is the formula for the surface area of a sphere. Choice (B) uses the information to generate an answer with the correct units, but without applying the equation for centripetal acceleration (although it includes π). This answer also represents the velocity, $\pi D/T$, rather than the acceleration. Choice (C) is incorrect because it uses an incorrect formula, $4\pi D^2$. This is the formula for the surface area of a sphere, but with the diameter in place of the radius. Choice (E) is incorrect because it uses the diameter instead of the radius in the equation for acceleration.

15

The diagram below shows a planet with a very eccentric orbit around a star. The planet's orbit is in the plane of the page. The planet was observed seven times over several months. The planet was first observed at point T. It was observed again at point U, 50 days later. Which other two observations could be 50 days apart?

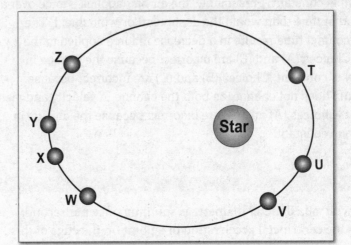

A) V and W

B) W and Y

C) X and Y

D) X and Z

E) Y and Z

Choice (C) is the correct answer. Satellites travel fastest when they are closest to the body they orbit. In this case, the planet is traveling fastest between points T and U and slowest at point Y. The distance between X and Y is much shorter than the distance between T and U, so it could take the planet the same amount of time to travel between points T and U as between points X and Y. Further, Kepler's second law of planetary motion states that satellites sweep out equal areas in equal amounts of time. The area of the sector between T, U and the star seems about equal to the area between X, Y and the star. Therefore, it could take the same amount of time to travel from T to U as from X to Y. Choices (A) and (D) represent distances that are the same as or longer than the distance between points T and U. Because these points are all farther from the star, the time for the planet to travel between each pair would be longer than 50 days. Choices (B) and (E) would sweep out larger areas than T to U, even though they are the same or shorter in distance than T to U; therefore, the time for the planet to travel between each pair would be longer than 50 days.

16

A 20-μF capacitor has a 30-V potential difference across it. What is the charge on the capacitor in coulombs?

A) 6.7×10^{-7} C

B) 6.0×10^{-4} C

C) 1.5 C

D) 6.0×10^{2} C

E) 1.5×10^{6} C

Choice (B) is the correct answer.

$C = q/\Delta V$ and $q = C \Delta V = (20 \times 10^{-6}$ F$) \times (30$ V$) = 6 \times 10^{-4}$ C

In this formula, C is capacitance, q is charge, and ΔV is the potential difference. Note that the unit C (not italicized) is coulomb. Choices (A) and (E) are incorrect because they use ratios of capacitance and potential difference rather than the product of these values. Choice (C) is incorrect for the same reason, and because the micro (μ) part of μF has been ignored. Choice (D) is incorrect because the micro (μ) part of μF has been ignored.

17

A 4.0-μF parallel-plate capacitor has an electrical potential difference of 5.0 V. Which of the following changes would most likely increase the potential difference to 10.0 V?

A) Doubling the area of the capacitor plates

B) Doubling the charge on each plate

C) Decreasing the distance between the plates by half

D) Decreasing the charge on each plate by half

E) Decreasing the time taken to charge the capacitor by half

Choice (B) is the correct answer. The parallel-plate capacitor is composed of two oppositely charged parallel plates. As the charge across the capacitor increases, the positive plate becomes more positively charged and the negative plate becomes more negatively charged. This results in a greater potential difference across the plates, since the positive plate will be at a higher potential and the negative plate will be at a lower potential. The relationship between capacitance, charge and potential difference is quantified in the formula $C = q/\Delta V$, where C is capacitance, q is charge, and V is potential difference. As shown below, increasing the potential difference from 5.0 V to 10.0 V is achieved through doubling the charge:

$$q_1 = C(\Delta V_1) = (4.0 \text{ μF})(5.0 \text{ V}) = 2.0 \times 10^{-5} \text{ C}$$

$$q_2 = C(\Delta V_2) = (4.0 \text{ μF})(10.0 \text{ V}) = 4.0 \times 10^{-5} \text{ C}$$

In the prior calculation, note that the unit C (not italicized) is the coulomb. Choices (A) and (C) are incorrect because these changes would require an entirely different capacitor and because larger capacitor plates or a shorter distance between them with an equal amount of charge would have a smaller potential difference. Choice (D) is incorrect because it would also result in a decrease rather than an increase in the potential difference. Choice (E) is incorrect because it would not affect the resulting potential difference.

18

A team of physics students is building a robot. They connect two motors to the parallel 6 volt circuit shown below. The arm motor uses 12 watts, and the wheel motor uses 18 watts. A student checks the current at three points in the circuit when both devices are in use. Which of the following lists these three points in order from lowest to highest current?

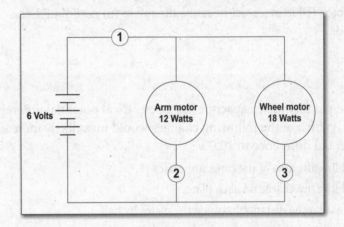

A) 1, 2, 3

B) 1, 3, 2

C) 2, 1, 3

D) 2, 3, 1

E) 3, 2, 1

Choice (D) is the correct answer. Current is equal to power divided by voltage, and in a parallel circuit, the current is equal to the sum of the currents in each branch. Therefore, the current is highest at point 1, and the current is greater at point 3 than at point 2. Choices (A), (B) and (C) are incorrect because the current in the circuit cannot be smaller than the current in any branch. Choice (E) is incorrect because it is the result of using an inverse, rather than a direct, relationship between current and power.

19

An incandescent light bulb uses the resistance of a tungsten filament to convert electrical energy into other forms of energy. If only about 10% of this energy is converted into visible light, how many kilojoules does a 100-watt light bulb give off in an hour in energy forms that we cannot see?

A) 36 kJ

B) 90 kJ

C) 324 kJ

D) 360 kJ

E) 32,400 kJ

Choice (C) is the correct answer. Power is the rate of energy use, so energy is then the product of power and time: E = (100 W)(3600 s) = 360,000 J = 360 kJ.

Because only 10% of this energy is converted to visible light, the remaining 90%, or 324 kJ, is converted to other forms of energy. Choice (A) is incorrect because 36 kJ is 10% of the energy that is visible light. Choice (B) is incorrect because it ignores the conversions of units from hours to seconds and joules to kilojoules. Choice (D) is incorrect because 360 kJ is 100% of the energy used. Choice (E) is incorrect because it uses the efficiency without converting from joules to kilojoules.

20

A beam of electrons passes through a magnetic field between two magnets resting on the table, as shown below.

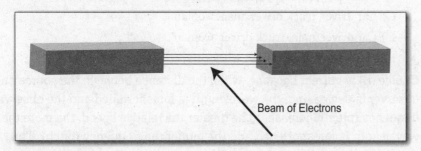

Beam of Electrons

How will the magnetic field affect the electron beam?

A) The beam will rotate around the two magnets.

B) The beam will bend up away from the table.

C) The beam will bend down into the table.

D) The beam will be attracted to the north pole of a magnet.

E) The beam will be attracted to the south pole of a magnet.

Choice (B) is the correct answer. The direction of electron flow is opposite the direction of conventional current. Either a right-hand rule can be applied with the thumb pointing opposite the direction of the beam of electrons or a left-hand rule can be applied with the thumb pointing in the direction of the beam of electrons. In either application, the fingers point in the direction of the magnetic field and the palm faces the direction of the force on the beam. Choice (A) is an incorrect application of a right-hand rule for magnetic fields. Choice (C) is incorrect because it reverses the direction of the applied force. Choices (D) and (E) are incorrect because they confound attraction between electrical charges with magnetic poles.

21

A fire truck is moving left with its siren on. A car is moving right, approaching the truck. A man is standing on the sidewalk to the left of the car, and a woman is standing on the sidewalk to the right of the truck. The truck driver, the car driver, the man and the woman all hear the siren as having a different pitch. Which of the following lists the people in order by the pitch they hear, from lowest pitch to highest pitch?

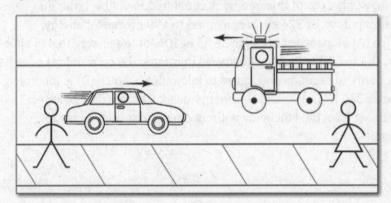

A) Truck driver, woman, man, car driver

B) Woman, truck driver, man, car driver

C) Car driver, truck driver, man, woman

D) Car driver, man, truck driver, woman

E) Man, woman, car driver, truck driver

Choice (B) is correct because, when the distance between the source and observer is decreasing, the wavelength is foreshortened and the observed frequency (pitch) increases. The greater the relative speed, the more the wavelength is foreshortened and the higher the frequency (pitch). The distance between the woman and the source of the sound is increasing because the truck is moving away (the observed frequency decreases). The truck driver's relative speed to the sound is zero. The man's relative speed to the sound is equal to the speed of the truck. The car driver's speed relative to the sound is greatest because it is the sum of his speed plus that of the truck.

22

The diagram below shows a beam of light passing through a piece of glass in water. The dashed lines are perpendicular to the surfaces of the glass. Which of the following describes the changes in the speed and frequency of the light as it passes through the glass?

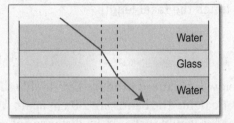

A) Both the frequency and speed of the light increase in the glass.

B) Both the frequency and speed of the light decrease in the glass.

C) The frequency increases but the speed of the light decreases in the glass.

D) The frequency decreases but the speed of the light stays constant in the glass.

E) The frequency stays constant but the speed of the light decreases in the glass.

Choice (E) is the correct answer. According to Snell's law, $\sin\Theta_1 / \sin\Theta_2 = v_1/v_2$, where Θ_1 and Θ_2 are the angles to the normal of the beam and v_1 and v_2 are velocities of mediums 1 and 2. For a beam of light incident on a surface, if the angle in the new medium is smaller, then the speed must have decreased. The frequency of light does not change in transparent media. Choices (A), (B), (C) and (D) are all incorrect because they state that the frequency of the light changes.

23

The diagram below shows how a concave mirror creates a real image of an object. The object is 20 cm from the mirror and the image appears at a distance of 5 cm from the mirror. What is the focal length of the mirror?

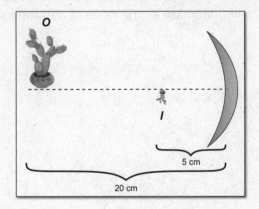

A) 2.5 cm

B) 4 cm

C) 25 cm

D) 20 cm

E) 40 cm

Choice (B) is the correct answer. Since $1/f = 1/d_o + 1/d_i$, then $f = d_i d_o / (d_o + d_i) = (5 \times 20)/(5 + 20) = 4$ cm, where f is the focal length, d_o is the distance of the object from the mirror, and d_i is the distance of the image from the mirror. Choices (A) and (C) could be the inverted formula with a misplaced decimal. Choice (C) is also the sum of the object and image distances. Choice (D) is the object distance. Choice (E) is 10 times the focal length.

24

The image below is a pattern produced by double slit diffraction of monochromatic light. The bands are 2.0 cm apart. Which of the following changes would increase the distance between the bands?

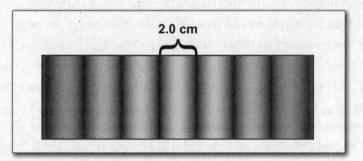

A) Moving the slits closer together

B) Making the light source brighter

C) Moving the slits closer to the screen

D) Increasing the frequency of the light

E) Shortening the wavelength of the light

Choice (A) is the correct answer. $\lambda = xd/L$, where λ is wavelength, x is the distance between bands, d is the distance between slits, and L is the distance to the screen. Moving the slits closer together will spread the diffraction pattern. Assuming the wavelength and distance L are constant, x will increase as the value of d in the formula decreases.

25

The table to the right lists several properties of water. Which of the following processes requires the most energy input?

Property	Value
Specific Heat	1.0 cal/g·°C
Latent Heat of Fusion	80 cal/g
Latent Heat of Vaporization	540 cal/g

A) Melting 100 g of ice at 0°C

B) Freezing 100 g of water at 0°C

C) Boiling 100 g of water at 100°C

D) Condensing 100 g of steam at 100°C

E) Heating 100 g of water from 0°C to 100°C

Choice (C) is the correct answer. The process of boiling 100 g of water at 100°C requires (540 cal/g) × 100 g = 54,000 calories of energy input. Choices (A) and (E) require less energy input. Melting 100 g of ice at 0°C requires (80 cal/g) × 100 g = 8,000 calories, and heating 100 g of water from 0°C to 100°C requires (1 cal/g·°C) × 100 g × 100°C = 10,000 calories. Choices (B) and (D) are incorrect because, rather than requiring an energy input, these processes result in an output of energy.

26

Ethanol melts at 156 K and has a latent heat of fusion of 25 cal/g. It requires 3,080 cal to raise 100 g of solid ethanol at 156 K to liquid ethanol at 166 K. What is the specific heat of ethanol?

A) 0.58 cal/g·K

B) 1.7 cal/g·K

C) 2.5 cal/g·K

D) 3.1 cal/g·K

E) 5.8 cal/g·K

Choice (A) is the correct answer. Total heat = heat to melt ethanol + heat to raise temperature. Then 3080 cal = $k_f m + c·m·\Delta T$ = 25 × 100 + c × 100 × 10, where k_f is the heat of fusion, c is the specific heat, m is mass, and ΔT is the change in temperature in kelvins. c = (3080 − 2500)/(10 × 100) = 0.58 cal/g·K. Choice (B) is the result of inverting the fraction. Choice (C) is 2500/(10 × 100). Choice (D) is 3080/(10 × 100). Choice (E) is the result of ignoring the rise in temperature.

27

The schematic below shows how energy is transferred in a refrigeration system. Which statement explains why work is an input into this system?

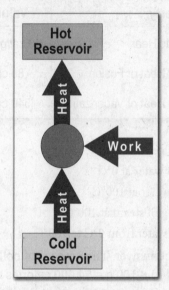

A) Work is needed to move thermal energy against a temperature gradient.

B) Work is needed to reduce the amount of thermal energy lost during transfer.

C) Work uses energy from the cold reservoir to reduce the temperature of the system.

D) Work adds energy to the cold reservoir to increase the heat flow to the hot reservoir.

E) Work adds heat to the system, causing the temperature of both reservoirs to increase.

Choice (A) is the correct answer. The heat pump works on the system by removing thermal energy from the cold reservoir (the inside of the refrigerator) and transferring it into the space outside the refrigerator (the hot reservoir). Choice (B) is incorrect because it incorrectly relates work and efficiency. Choice (C) is incorrect because the cold reservoir is not the source of energy for work. Choice (D) is incorrect because energy is not added to the cold reservoir. Choice (E) is incorrect because the temperature of the cold reservoir does not increase.

28

The principle of complementarity states that phenomena can have properties that are contradictory. These contradictory properties can be observed separately, but not simultaneously. Which of the following pairs of phenomena are examples of complementarity?

A) Mass and weight

B) Heat and temperature

C) Light waves and particles

D) Magnetic and electric fields

E) Frequency and intensity of sound

Choice (C) is the correct answer. Light has both the properties of waves (i.e., electromagnetic waves) and particles. For example, light demonstrates wave-like behavior as observed through the interference patterns formed in Young's double-slit experiment. However, light also exhibits particle-like behavior, which can be demonstrated by the photoelectric effect. These contradictory properties of light support the wave-particle duality of light. Light can exhibit wave and particle properties, but not at the same time. The other answer choices include pairs that are observed without the need to propose contradictory properties.

29

If m_p = the mass of a proton, m_n = the mass of a neutron, m_{He} = the mass of a helium nucleus, and c = the speed of light, the expression for the energy released during the formation of a helium nucleus is:

A) $E = \left[\left(2m_p + 2m_n\right) - m_{He}\right]c^2$

B) $E = \left(2m_p + 2m_n\right)c^2$

C) $E = m_{He}c^2$

D) $E = \left[\left(2m_p + 2m_n\right) - m_{He}\right]c$

E) $E = \left[m_{He} - \left(2m_p + 2m_n\right)\right]c^2$

Choice (A) is the correct answer. The binding energy is the energy equivalent of the mass difference between the nucleons and the nucleus. This mass is converted to energy when the nucleus is formed.
Choices (B) and (C) are the energy equivalents of the nucleons and nucleus, respectively. Choice (D) neglects to square c. Choice (E) is the negative of the correct answer.

30

The diagram below shows two forces acting on an object with magnitudes X and Y. The forces are perpendicular to each other. What is the magnitude of the net force acting on the object?

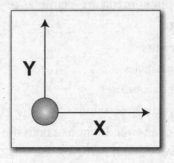

A) $X - Y$

B) $X + Y$

C) $\sqrt{X-Y}$

D) $\sqrt{X^2-Y^2}$

E) $\sqrt{X^2+Y^2}$

Choice (E) is the correct answer. The resultant force, R, is the hypotenuse of the right triangle with X as the adjacent side and Y as the opposite side. The magnitude of the net force can be found using the Pythagorean theorem, $R^2 = X^2 + Y^2$, where R, X and Y are the magnitudes of vectors R, X and Y. Choices (A) and (B) could be solutions to vector addition in one dimension. Choices (C) and (D) misinterpret the Pythagorean theorem.

Physics Subject Test - Practice Test 1

Practice Helps

The test that follows is an actual, previously administered SAT Subject Test in Physics. To get an idea of what it's like to take this test, practice under conditions that are much like those of an actual test administration.

- Set aside an hour when you can take the test uninterrupted.

- Sit at a desk or table with no other books or papers. Dictionaries, other books, or notes are not allowed in the test room.

- Do not use a calculator. Calculators are not allowed for the Subject Test in Physics.

- Tear out an answer sheet from the back of this book and fill it in just as you would on the day of the test. One answer sheet can be used for up to three Subject Tests.

- Read the instructions that precede the practice test. During the actual administration you will be asked to read them before answering test questions.

- Time yourself by placing a clock or kitchen timer in front of you.

- After you finish the practice test, read the sections "How to Score the SAT Subject Test in Physics" and "How Did You Do on the Subject Test in Physics?"

- The appearance of the answer sheet in this book may differ from the answer sheet you see on test day.

PHYSICS TEST

The top portion of the page of the answer sheet that you will use in taking the Physics Test must be filled in exactly as illustrated below. When your supervisor tells you to fill in the circle next to the name of the test you are about to take, mark your answer sheet as shown.

◯ Literature	◯ Mathematics Level 1	◯ German	◯ Chinese Listening	◯ Japanese Listening
◯ Biology E	◯ Mathematics Level 2	◯ Italian	◯ French Listening	◯ Korean Listening
◯ Biology M	◯ U.S. History	◯ Latin	◯ German Listening	◯ Spanish Listening
◯ Chemistry	◯ World History	◯ Modern Hebrew		
● Physics	◯ French	◯ Spanish	**Background Questions:** ① ② ③ ④ ⑤ ⑥ ⑦ ⑧ ⑨

After filling in the circle next to the name of the test you are taking, locate the Background Questions section, which also appears at the top of your answer sheet (as shown above). This is where you will answer the following Background Questions on your answer sheet.

BACKGROUND QUESTIONS

Please answer the three questions below by filling in the appropriate circle in the Background Questions box on your answer sheet. The information you provide is for statistical purposes only and will not affect your test score.

Question 1

How many semesters of physics have you taken in high school, including any semester in which you are currently enrolled? (Count as two semesters any case in which a full year's course is taught in a one-semester [half-year] compressed schedule.) Fill in only one circle of circles 1-3.

- One semester or less   —Fill in circle 1.
- Two semesters   —Fill in circle 2.
- Three semesters or more   —Fill in circle 3.

Question 2

About how often did you do lab work in your first physics course? (Include any times when you may have watched a film or a demonstration by your teacher and then discussed or analyzed data.) Fill in only one circle of circles 4-7.

- Less than once a week   —Fill in circle 4.
- About once a week   —Fill in circle 5.
- A few times a week   —Fill in circle 6.
- Almost every day   —Fill in circle 7.

Question 3

If you have taken or are currently taking an Advanced Placement (AP) Physics course, which of the following describes the course? Fill in both circles if applicable. (If you have never had AP Physics, leave circles 8 and 9 blank.)

- A course that uses algebra and trigonometry but NOT calculus (Physics 1 and/or Physics 2)   —Fill in circle 8.
- A course that uses calculus (Physics C)   —Fill in circle 9.

When the supervisor gives the signal, turn the page and begin the Physics Test. There are 100 numbered circles on the answer sheet and 75 questions in the Physics Test. Therefore, use only circles 1 to 75 for recording your answers.

PHYSICS TEST

Note: To simplify calculations, you may use $g = 10 \text{ m/s}^2$ for the acceleration due to gravity at Earth's surface.

Part A

Directions: Each set of lettered choices below refers to the numbered questions immediately following it. Select the one lettered choice that best answers each question, and then fill in the corresponding circle on the answer sheet. A choice may be used once, more than once, or not at all in each set.

Questions 1-2

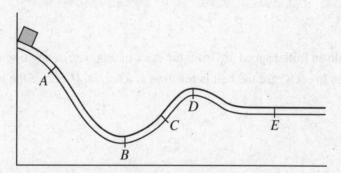

The figure above represents a track on which an object slides without friction. The object is released from the top of the track in the position shown.

(A) Point A
(B) Point B
(C) Point C
(D) Point D
(E) Point E

1. At which of the labeled points is the object's potential energy greatest?

2. At which of the labeled points is the object's kinetic energy greatest?

GO ON TO THE NEXT PAGE

Questions 3-6

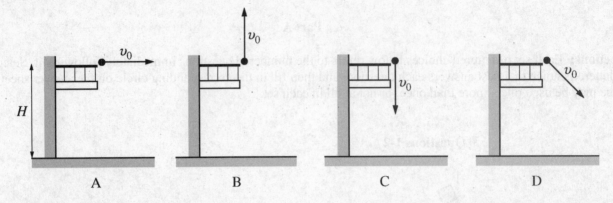

A   B   C   D

A person throws a ball with an initial speed v_0 from the deck of a house, in any one of the four initial directions shown in the diagrams above. In each case the ball is released at a height H above the ground. Air resistance is negligible.

(A) A only
(B) B only
(C) C only
(D) D only
(E) It is the same for all four cases.

3. In which case does the ball travel the greatest horizontal distance before hitting the ground?

4. In which case does the ball have the greatest speed when it hits the ground?

5. In which case does the ball have the greatest acceleration just before it hits the ground?

6. In which case is the ball in the air for the longest time?

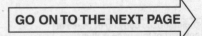
GO ON TO THE NEXT PAGE

Questions 7-8 refer to the following properties of light waves.

    I. Frequency
    II. Wavelength
    III. Speed

(A) I only
(B) III only
(C) I and II only
(D) II and III only
(E) I, II, and III

7. In a vacuum, all colors of light have the same value for which of the properties?

8. When light passes from air into glass, which of the properties changes?

Questions 9-10

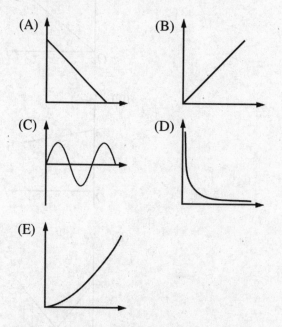

A block on a frictionless tabletop is attached to a horizontal spring that is fixed to a wall, as shown above. The block is pulled to the right. Choose answers to the following questions from the set of graphs below.

9. Which graph represents the magnitude of the linear restoring force as a function of the block's displacement from its equilibrium position?

10. Which graph represents the elastic potential energy stored in the spring as a function of the block's displacement from equilibrium?

GO ON TO THE NEXT PAGE

Questions 11-12

A particle moves along the x axis and is acted on by a net force directed along the line of motion. Possible graphs of velocity v_x as a function of time t are shown below. All graphs are drawn to the same scale.

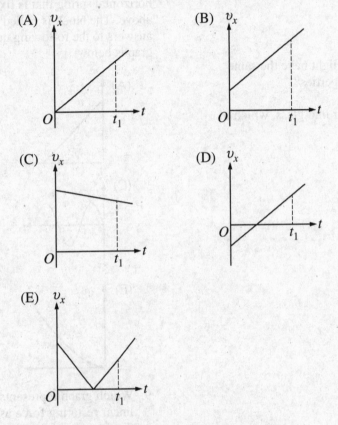

11. Which graph is NOT possible for a force that is constant in magnitude and direction?

12. Which graph describes a situation in which the velocity of the particle changes direction between $t = 0$ and $t = t_1$?

GO ON TO THE NEXT PAGE

Questions 13-15

The following diagrams each represent an isolated charge $+Q$ at the center of the circle shown. In each case, a test charge $+q$ is moved from rest at X to rest at Y by an external force along the path shown.

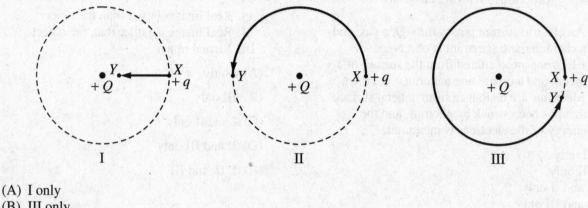

      I   II   III

(A) I only
(B) III only
(C) I and II only
(D) II and III only
(E) I, II, and III

13. The net work done by the external force is maximum in which of these cases?

14. No net work is done by the external force in which of these cases?

15. The electric potential at Y is higher than at X in which of these cases?

GO ON TO THE NEXT PAGE

Questions 16-17

The statements below describe experimental observations of processes involving electrons.

    I. An electric current passes through a gas, and a characteristic spectrum is observed.

    II. Electrons are scattered from the surface of a metal, and a diffraction pattern is observed.

    III. Electrons are dislodged from a metal surface that has been struck by photons, and the energy of the electrons is measured.

(A) II only
(B) III only
(C) I and II only
(D) I and III only
(E) I, II, and III

16. Evidence for the particle nature of light is provided by which of the observations?

17. Evidence that an electron needs a minimum energy to leave a surface is provided by which of the observations?

Questions 18-19 refer to the following types of images that may be formed when an object is placed in front of a lens or mirror.

    I. Real image, larger than the object
    II. Real image, smaller than the object
    III. Virtual image

(A) I only

(B) III only

(C) I and II only

(D) II and III only

(E) I, II, and III

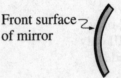

Front surface of mirror

18. Which of these types of images can be formed by the convex mirror shown above?

19. Which of these types of images can be formed by the converging lens shown above?

GO ON TO THE NEXT PAGE

Questions 20-21

Standing waves are produced on the strings of a guitar. The following represent possible comparisons of the fundamental frequency and the fundamental wavelength of the waves when a change is made.

	Frequency	Wavelength
(A)	Lower	Longer
(B)	Lower	Stays the same
(C)	Stays the same	Shorter
(D)	Higher	Shorter
(E)	Higher	Stays the same

For each of the following situations, indicate how the second standing wave compares to the first standing wave.

20. The guitarist first plucks a thin string and then a thick string, where both strings are the same length and under the same tension.

21. The guitarist plucks a string, then tightens it and plucks it again.

GO ON TO THE NEXT PAGE

Part B

Directions: Each of the questions or incomplete statements below is followed by five suggested answers or completions. Select the one that is best in each case and then fill in the corresponding circle on the answer sheet.

22. Which of the following is a correct unit for the coefficient of friction μ ?

    (A) Newton
    (B) Kilogram
    (C) Newton/kilogram
    (D) Kilogram/newton
    (E) No unit; μ is a dimensionless quantity.

23. A rocket-powered sled is accelerating along a straight, level track with a constant acceleration of magnitude 20 meters per second squared. By how much will the speed of the sled change in 3.00 seconds?

    (A) 7 m/s
    (B) 10 m/s
    (C) 20 m/s
    (D) 60 m/s
    (E) 90 m/s

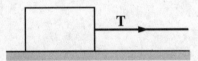

24. The block shown above is pulled over a rough horizontal surface by the tension force **T** in the string. The velocity of the block does not change and therefore it may be correctly inferred that

    (A) the inertial mass of the block is infinite
    (B) the inertial mass of the block is zero
    (C) the force due to friction and the tension are equal in magnitude
    (D) the block will continue to move at a constant velocity if **T** is reduced to zero
    (E) this constant velocity condition can be maintained by a tension of any desired value

25. A 2-kilogram box is placed on a scale in an elevator. When the elevator is not moving, the reading on the scale is 20 newtons. When the elevator is accelerating upward at 2 m/s², the reading on the scale will be most nearly

    (A) 40 N
    (B) 24 N
    (C) 18 N
    (D) 17 N
    (E) 4 N

26. The observation of diffraction patterns produced when monochromatic light is incident on narrow slits provides evidence for which of the following?

    (A) The particle nature of light
    (B) The wave nature of light
    (C) Polarization
    (D) The law of reflection
    (E) The law of refraction

27. The phenomenon responsible for the separation of colors in the formation of a rainbow is also the cause of which of the following?

    (A) Colors in a thin soap film
    (B) Colors on a printed page
    (C) The colors seen on a compact disc (CD)
    (D) Spectra observed with diffraction gratings
    (E) The spectrum formed by a glass prism

GO ON TO THE NEXT PAGE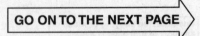

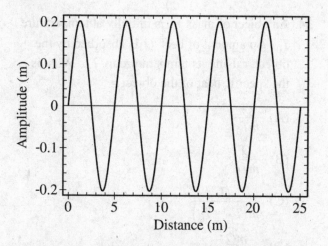

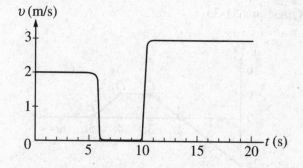

28. A small cork moves under the influence of a water wave, whose shape at a particular time is shown in the graph above. If the wave has a speed of 2.0 meters per second, how long does it take for the cork to make one complete oscillation?

    (A) 12.5 s
    (B) 10 s
    (C)   5.0 s
    (D)   2.5 s
    (E)   0.40 s

29. An astronaut is on a planet whose mass is twice the mass of Earth and whose diameter is the same as Earth's diameter. The astronaut's weight on this planet is

    (A) four times what it is on Earth
    (B) twice what it is on Earth
    (C) the same as it is on Earth
    (D) one-half what it is on Earth
    (E) one-quarter what it is on Earth

30. A toy train undergoes three periods of constant speed, as shown in the graph above: 6 seconds moving at 2 meters per second, 4 seconds standing still, and 10 seconds moving at 3 meters per second. The average speed of the train for these 20 seconds is most nearly

    (A) 2.1 m/s
    (B) 2.4 m/s
    (C) 2.5 m/s
    (D) 2.6 m/s
    (E) 3.2 m/s

GO ON TO THE NEXT PAGE

Questions 31-33

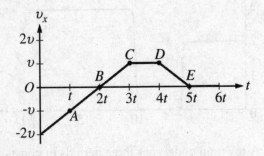

Velocity v_x versus time t for an object moving along the x axis is graphed above.

31. The object is instantaneously at rest for which of the points?

   (A) None
   (B) B only
   (C) C only
   (D) B and E
   (E) C and D

32. The magnitude of the object's acceleration is a minimum in the region between which two points?

   (A) A and B only
   (B) B and C only
   (C) A and C
   (D) C and D
   (E) D and E

33. At which point is the object the greatest <u>distance</u> from its position at $t = 0$?

   (A) A
   (B) B
   (C) C
   (D) D
   (E) E

34. An object of mass m is initially at temperature T_0. An amount of heat Q is absorbed by the object, raising its temperature to T_f. What is the specific heat of the object?

   (A) $\dfrac{Q}{mT_0}$

   (B) $\dfrac{Q}{mT_f}$

   (C) $\dfrac{Q}{m\left(T_f - T_0\right)}$

   (D) $\dfrac{mQ}{T_f - T_0}$

   (E) $\dfrac{mQ}{T_f}$

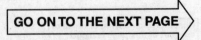
GO ON TO THE NEXT PAGE

Questions 35-37

A heat engine is represented in the figure below. During each cycle the engine absorbs 600 joules of thermal energy from the heat source and exhausts 500 joules of thermal energy to the heat sink.

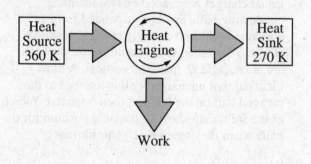

35. How much work is done by the engine during each cycle?

   (A)   100 J
   (B)   500 J
   (C)   550 J
   (D)   600 J
   (E) 1,100 J

36. If the engine operates at 20 cycles per second and does X joules of work during each cycle, which of the following is an expression for the power generated by the engine?

   (A) $\dfrac{X}{20}$ watts

   (B) $\dfrac{20}{X}$ watts

   (C) $\dfrac{(20)(X)}{60}$ watts

   (D) $(20)(X)$ watts

   (E) $(20)(60)(X)$ watts

37. If the temperatures of the heat source and heat sink are 360 K and 270 K, respectively, what is the theoretical (ideal) maximum efficiency of the engine?

   (A)   17%
   (B)   25%
   (C)   36%
   (D)   75%
   (E) 100%

Questions 38-39

The figure above depicts a thick glass mug initially at room temperature in which a sensitive liquid-in-glass thermometer has been placed. A student pours very hot water into the mug.

38. The student carefully observes the reading on the thermometer and sees that it initially drops and then gradually rises. The student's observations can be explained by which of the following?

   (A) The liquid in the thermometer contracts and then expands.
   (B) The glass of the thermometer contracts and then expands.
   (C) The thermometer glass expands after the liquid inside it expands.
   (D) The thermometer glass expands before the liquid inside it expands.
   (E) None of the above

39. Soon after the hot water is poured into the glass mug, the mug cracks open. This is most likely due to which of the following?

   (A) The outer wall of the mug expands before the inner wall does.
   (B) The inner wall of the mug expands before the outer wall does.
   (C) The outer wall of the mug contracts before the inner wall does.
   (D) The inner wall of the mug contracts before the outer wall does.
   (E) The hot water puts pressure on the mug.

GO ON TO THE NEXT PAGE

40. Two samples of an element are prepared, each containing a different isotope of that element. Which of the following properties of individual neutral atoms is NOT the same for both samples?

    (A) Atomic mass
    (B) Atomic number
    (C) Number of protons
    (D) Number of valence electrons
    (E) Total number of electrons

41. A spaceship is traveling toward the Earth at a speed of 2×10^8 meters per second when it fires a laser pulse directly at the Earth. What will observers on Earth measure the speed of the laser pulse to be?

    (A) 1.0×10^8 m/s
    (B) 2.0×10^8 m/s
    (C) 2.5×10^8 m/s
    (D) 3.0×10^8 m/s
    (E) 5.0×10^8 m/s

42. According to present experimental evidence, which of the following is true of protons and electrons?

    (A) Their charges are of the same sign.
    (B) They have the same mass.
    (C) They are not known to decay.
    (D) They are both made of quarks.
    (E) They are about the same size.

43. Correct statements about atomic nuclei include which of the following?

    I. Two nuclei with the same charge contain the same number of protons.
    II. Nuclei are positively charged.
    III. The nucleus contains a small fraction of the mass of an atom.

    (A) I only
    (B) III only
    (C) I and II only
    (D) II and III only
    (E) I, II, and III

44. Equal charges are placed on two identical conducting balls that are suspended from a common point by very long strings, as shown above. When they reach equilibrium, the balls are at an angle θ from the vertical. A third identical, but uncharged ball is touched to the charged ball on the left and then removed. Which of the following shows a possible position for the balls when they again reach equilibrium?

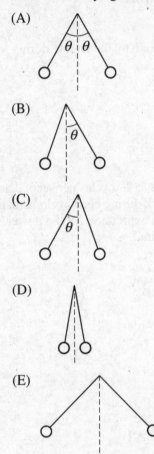

GO ON TO THE NEXT PAGE

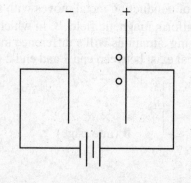

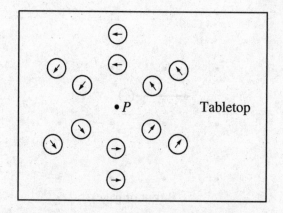

45. Two charged particles in a uniform electric field between two large parallel plates are at the positions shown above when they are simultaneously released from rest. If the two particles reach the negative plate at the same time, one can definitely conclude that they have the same

    (A) charge only
    (B) mass only
    (C) charge and mass
    (D) product of charge and mass
    (E) ratio of charge to mass

46. The force on a straight current-carrying wire in a magnetic field that is perpendicular to the wire depends on which of the following?

    I. Strength of the magnetic field
    II. Current in the wire
    III. Length of the wire in the field

    (A) I only
    (B) III only
    (C) I and II only
    (D) II and III only
    (E) I, II, and III

47. A number of small magnetic compasses on a wood tabletop are oriented as shown above. These compasses are most likely situated

    (A) around a current-carrying wire passing perpendicularly through a hole in the table at point P
    (B) between two magnetic poles, a north pole directly above the table from point P and a south pole directly beneath point P
    (C) between two magnetic poles, a south pole directly above the table from point P and a north pole directly beneath point P
    (D) in a uniform magnetic field parallel to the tabletop and directed to the right
    (E) in a uniform magnetic field parallel to the tabletop and directed to the left

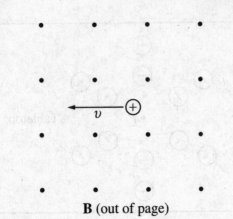

B (out of page)

48. A positively charged particle moves to the left through a magnetic field B that is directed out of the page, as shown above. What is the direction of the force exerted on the particle by the magnetic field?

   (A) Toward the left
   (B) Toward the right
   (C) Toward the top of the page
   (D) Into the page
   (E) Out of the page

49. Which of the following statements is true of a transformer?

   (A) It uses an iron core to reduce the magnetic flux linkages between the primary and secondary coils.
   (B) The voltage induced in the secondary coil is due to the changing magnetic flux set up by a changing current in the primary coil.
   (C) It is a DC device that is based on a resistor used to control current.
   (D) It is an AC device that is based on a capacitor used to control voltage.
   (E) It is an electric motor run backward.

50. A bar of conducting metal moves with speed v in a uniform magnetic field **B**. In which of the following situations will a difference in electrical potential exist between end 1 and end 2 of the bar?

   (A)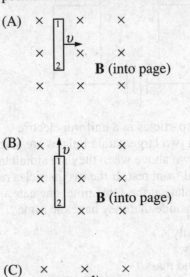

   (B)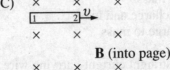

   (C)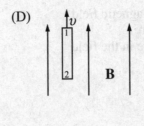

   (D)

   (E)

GO ON TO THE NEXT PAGE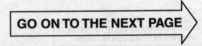

51. Why does our calendar usually include a leap year every four years?

    (A) The Moon's orbit around Earth is an ellipse, so it causes Earth to wobble.
    (B) The period of Earth's orbit is not an integer multiple of the period of Earth's rotation on its axis.
    (C) As other planets pass by Earth, they cause a continual decrease in Earth's orbital speed.
    (D) The period of Earth's orbit changes because its orbit is elliptical.
    (E) Friction due to tides causes Earth to rotate faster on its axis.

52. In some designs for high-speed, magnetically levitated trains, there are superconducting electromagnets in the bottom of each car. This design is chosen because, when compared to conventional electromagnets, superconducting electromagnets

    (A) use less electrical power
    (B) are less expensive to manufacture
    (C) operate at cooler temperatures
    (D) allow the train to run more smoothly over the track
    (E) decrease the magnetic field required to levitate the train

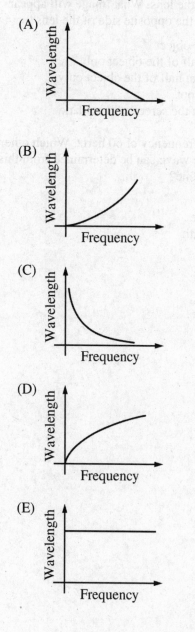

53. The wavelength of a wave is plotted versus its period on the graph above. Which of the following graphs best represents the wavelength versus the frequency?

Unauthorized copying or reuse of any part of this page is illegal.

GO ON TO THE NEXT PAGE

57

54. The speed of light in a glass prism varies with the

   (A) frequency of the light
   (B) angle of incidence
   (C) intensity of the light source
   (D) distance between the light source and the prism
   (E) polarization of the light

55. The bottom half of a converging lens is covered so that light from an object can only pass through the top half of the lens. What image will appear on a screen on the opposite side of the lens?

   (A) The entire object
   (B) The top half of the object only
   (C) The bottom half of the object only
   (D) A bright spot
   (E) No image; the screen will be dark.

56. A wave has a frequency of 60 hertz. Which other property of the wave can be determined from this information alone?

   (A) Speed
   (B) Amplitude
   (C) Wavelength
   (D) Period
   (E) Intensity

Questions 57-58

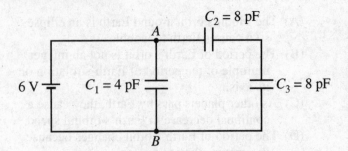

In an experiment, a student has connected three initially uncharged capacitors and a battery, as shown in the figure above.

57. What is the equivalent capacitance of the circuit between points A and B ?

   (A) 3.2 pF
   (B) 4.0 pF
   (C) 5.8 pF
   (D) 8.0 pF
   (E) 20 pF

58. What are the voltages across the capacitors after equilibrium has been reached?

	C_1	C_2	C_3
(A)	3 V	6 V	3 V
(B)	3 V	6 V	6 V
(C)	6 V	3 V	3 V
(D)	6 V	6 V	6 V
(E)	6 V	12 V	12 V

GO ON TO THE NEXT PAGE

Questions 59-60

To confirm Ohm's law, an experiment is performed with a battery, an ammeter, a voltmeter, a fixed-value resistor, and a variable resistor.

59. Which of the following circuits would allow you to take appropriate measurements to verify Ohm's law?

(A)
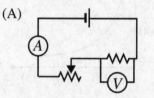

(B)
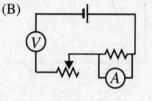

(C)
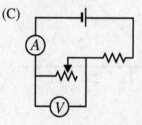

(D)
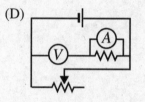

(E)
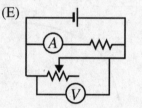

GO ON TO THE NEXT PAGE

60. If R is resistance, V is voltage, and I is current, which of the following shows a relationship between the graphed quantities that is consistent with Ohm's law? (In each case, assume the third quantity is held constant.)

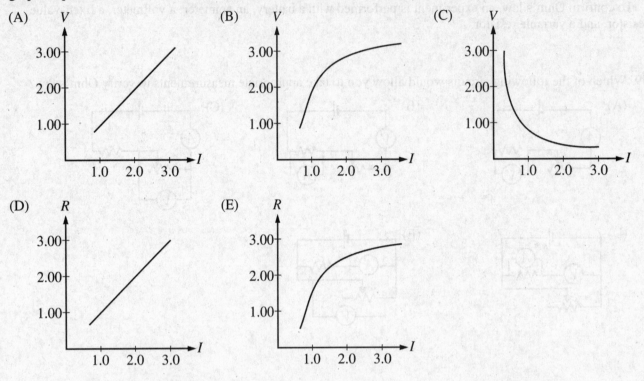

GO ON TO THE NEXT PAGE

61. To determine the power dissipated by a resistor, a student obtained the following data.

    Potential difference across resistor:
         10.0 volts ± 5%
    Current through resistor:
         2.0 amperes ± 25%

    If the power is expressed as 20 watts ± x%, x is most nearly

    (A) 15%
    (B) 20%
    (C) 25%
    (D) 30%
    (E) 125%

62. A steel spring with nonzero mass has zero elastic potential energy when no forces are exerted on it. A mass is attached to one end of the spring and allowed to oscillate on a horizontal, frictionless tabletop. True statements about the spring include which of the following?

    I. When the spring is compressed, it will have elastic potential energy greater than zero.
    II. When the spring is stretched, it will have elastic potential energy greater than zero.
    III. The spring will always have zero kinetic energy.

    (A) I only
    (B) II only
    (C) III only
    (D) I and II only
    (E) I, II, and III

Questions 63-64

A foam ball is dropped from a tall tower. Assume that there is no wind but that air resistance is directly proportional to the ball's speed.

63. Which of the following is true about the ball's motion for a short time after it is released?

    (A) Its potential energy remains constant.
    (B) Its speed decreases.
    (C) Its acceleration decreases.
    (D) Its acceleration is constant but not zero.
    (E) Its acceleration is zero.

64. When the air resistance on the ball equals the force of gravity on it, the ball has a constant

    (A) velocity
    (B) total energy (potential and kinetic)
    (C) nonzero net force acting on it
    (D) acceleration of magnitude greater than zero but less than g
    (E) acceleration of magnitude equal to g

GO ON TO THE NEXT PAGE

65. Which of the following describes the conditions under which the total momentum of a system of particles is conserved?

   (A) Only whenever energy is also conserved
   (B) Only whenever no net external force acts on the system
   (C) Only whenever no net internal force acts on the system
   (D) Only whenever the particles collide elastically
   (E) Only whenever the particles collide inelastically

66. What is the centripetal force on an object of mass 4 kilograms traveling in a circular path with a radius of 20 meters at a speed of 2 meters per second?

   (A) 160 N
   (B) 40 N
   (C) 5 N
   (D) 0.8 N
   (E) 0.1 N

67. In an electron microscope, the beam of electrons is focused by

   (A) gravitational forces
   (B) magnetic fields
   (C) a glass lens
   (D) a particle accelerator
   (E) semiconductor diodes

Questions 68-69

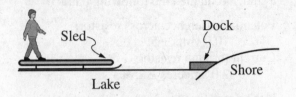

A person stands on a sled on a frozen lake. The friction between the sled and the ice is negligible. Initially, the person and the sled are motionless. The person then walks on the sled toward a dock, as shown above.

68. While the person is walking on the sled, how do the person and the sled each move with respect to the dock?

	Person	Sled
(A)	Toward the dock	Toward the dock
(B)	Toward the dock	Away from the dock
(C)	Toward the dock	Does not move
(D)	Does not move	Toward the dock
(E)	Does not move	Does not move

69. Before reaching the end of the sled, the person stops walking. Which of the following describes the velocity of the person and the sled with respect to the dock after the person has stopped walking?

	Person	Sled
(A)	Zero	Zero
(B)	Zero	Away from the dock
(C)	Away from the dock	Toward the dock
(D)	Toward the dock	Away from the dock
(E)	Toward the dock	Toward the dock

GO ON TO THE NEXT PAGE

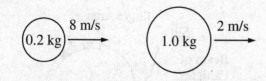

70. A 0.2-kilogram disk sliding at 8 meters per second on a table with negligible friction, as shown above, strikes a 1.0-kilogram disk sliding at 2 meters per second in the same direction. After the collision, the 0.2-kilogram disk slides backward at 2 meters per second. What is the speed of the 1.0-kilogram disk after the collision?

    (A) 1.2 m/s
    (B) 2.0 m/s
    (C) 3.2 m/s
    (D) 4.0 m/s
    (E) 8.0 m/s

71. At the instant shown in the following diagrams, an object that is moving horizontally to the right with velocity **v** is acted on by a net force **F**. In which of these cases is the kinetic energy of the object not changing?

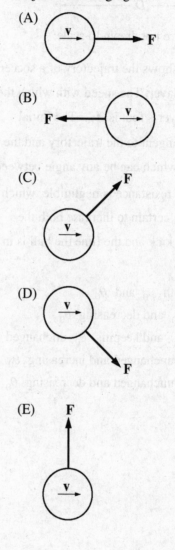

Unauthorized copying or reuse of any part of this page is illegal.

GO ON TO THE NEXT PAGE

63

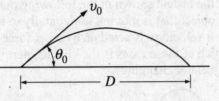

Note: Figure not drawn to scale.

72. The figure above shows the trajectory of a soccer ball kicked by a player. The speed with which the ball leaves the player's foot is v_0. The initial angle between a tangent to the trajectory and the horizontal is θ_0, which can be any angle between $0°$ and $90°$. If air resistance is negligible, which of the following is certain to increase both the distance D of the kick and the time the ball is in the air?

(A) Increasing both v_0 and θ_0
(B) Increasing v_0 and decreasing θ_0
(C) Increasing v_0 and keeping θ_0 unchanged
(D) Keeping v_0 unchanged and increasing θ_0
(E) Keeping v_0 unchanged and decreasing θ_0

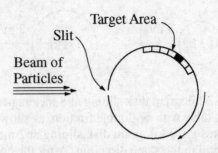

73. Particles enter a slit in a rotating drum of known diameter and rotation speed, as shown above. They strike the darkened region of the target inside the drum, which is at a known angle from the slit. With no additional data, this experiment can be used to determine which of the following properties of the particles?

(A) Mass
(B) Speed
(C) Charge
(D) Momentum
(E) Energy

GO ON TO THE NEXT PAGE

74. Two planets that are far apart have the same mass, but planet Y has a radius 3 times that of planet X, as shown above. If a is the magnitude of the acceleration due to gravity on the surface of planet X, what is the magnitude of the acceleration due to gravity on the surface of planet Y?

    (A) $9a$

    (B) $3a$

    (C) a

    (D) $a/3$

    (E) $a/9$

75. A car is being pushed up a hill and moves with constant velocity. What is the direction of the net force acting on the car?

    (A) Up the hill in the direction of the push
    (B) Down the hill in the direction of the frictional force
    (C) Perpendicular to the hill in the direction of the normal force
    (D) Straight down in the direction of the gravitational force
    (E) The net force has no direction because it is zero.

STOP

IF YOU FINISH BEFORE TIME IS CALLED, YOU MAY CHECK YOUR WORK ON THIS TEST ONLY. DO NOT TURN TO ANY OTHER TEST IN THIS BOOK.

How to Score the SAT Subject Test in Physics

When you take an actual SAT Subject Test in Physics, your answer sheet will be "read" by a scanning machine that will record your response to each question. Then a computer will compare your answers with the correct answers and produce your raw score. You get one point for each correct answer. For each wrong answer, you lose one-fourth of a point. Questions you omit (and any for which you mark more than one answer) are not counted. This raw score is converted to a scaled score that is reported to you and to the colleges you specify.

Worksheet 1. Finding Your Raw Test Score

STEP 1: Table A on the following page lists the correct answers for all the questions on the Subject Test in Physics that is reproduced in this book. It also serves as a worksheet for you to calculate your raw score.

- Compare your answers with those given in the table.

- Put a check in the column marked "Right" if your answer is correct.

- Put a check in the column marked "Wrong" if your answer is incorrect.

- Leave both columns blank if you omitted the question.

STEP 2: Count the number of right answers.

Enter the total here: _____

STEP 3: Count the number of wrong answers.

Enter the total here: _____

STEP 4: Multiply the number of wrong answers by .250.

Enter the product here: _____

STEP 5: Subtract the result obtained in Step 4 from the total you obtained in Step 2.

Enter the result here: _____

STEP 6: Round the number obtained in Step 5 to the nearest whole number.

Enter the result here: _____

The number you obtained in Step 6 is your raw score.

Answers to Practice Test 1

Table A

Answers to the Subject Test in Physics - Practice Test 1 and Percentage of Students Answering Each Question Correctly

Question Number	Correct Answer	Right	Wrong	Percent Answering Correctly*	Question Number	Correct Answer	Right	Wrong	Percent Answering Correctly*
1	A			92	26	B			65
2	B			89	27	E			75
3	A			93	28	D			66
4	E			20	29	B			78
5	E			66	30	A			72
6	B			91	31	D			74
7	B			72	32	D			74
8	D			58	33	B			39
9	B			53	34	C			76
10	E			56	35	A			75
11	E			80	36	D			60
12	D			70	37	B			43
13	A			63	38	D			47
14	D			53	39	B			73
15	A			71	40	A			70
16	B			31	41	D			42
17	B			71	42	C			35
18	B			57	43	C			66
19	E			41	44	D			53
20	B			25	45	E			34
21	E			23	46	E			63
22	E			83	47	A			67
23	D			89	48	C			69
24	C			81	49	B			38
25	B			69	50	A			36

Table A continued on next page

Table A continued from previous page

Question Number	Correct Answer	Right	Wrong	Percent Answering Correctly*	Question Number	Correct Answer	Right	Wrong	Percent Answering Correctly*
51	B			60	66	D			72
52	A			29	67	B			42
53	C			50	68	B			69
54	A			48	69	A			34
55	A			36	70	D			46
56	D			76	71	E			64
57	D			44	72	C			57
58	C			47	73	B			45
59	A			43	74	E			60
60	A			76	75	E			62
61	D			38					
62	D			57					
63	C			33					
64	A			71					
65	B			49					

* These percentages are based on an analysis of the answer sheets for a random sample of 9,251 students who took the original administration of this test and whose mean score was 661. They may be used as an indication of the relative difficulty of a particular question. Each percentage may also be used to predict the likelihood that a typical Subject Test in Physics candidate will answer correctly that question on this edition of this test.

Note: Answer explanations can be found on page 72.

Finding Your Scaled Score

When you take SAT Subject Tests, the scores sent to the colleges you specify are reported on the College Board scale, which ranges from 200 to 800. You can convert your practice test score to a scaled score by using Table B. To find your scaled score, locate your raw score in the left-hand column of Table B; the corresponding score in the right-hand column is your scaled score. For example, a raw score of 38 on this particular edition of the Subject Test in Physics corresponds to a scaled score of 670.

Raw scores are converted to scaled scores to ensure that a score earned on any one edition of a particular Subject Test is comparable to the same scaled score earned on any other edition of the same Subject Test. Because some editions of the tests may be slightly easier or more difficult than others, College Board scaled scores are adjusted so that they indicate the same level of performance regardless of the edition of the test taken and the ability of the group that takes it. Thus, for example, a score of 400 on one edition of a test taken at a particular administration indicates the same level of achievement as a score of 400 on a different edition of the test taken at a different administration.

When you take the SAT Subject Tests during a national administration, your scores are likely to differ somewhat from the scores you obtain on the tests in this book. People perform at different levels at different times for reasons unrelated to the tests themselves. The precision of any test is also limited because it represents only a sample of all the possible questions that could be asked.

Table B
Scaled Score Conversion Table
Subject Test in Physics - Practice Test 1

Raw Score	Scaled Score	Raw Score	Scaled Score	Raw Score	Scaled Score
75	800	35	650	−5	360
74	800	34	640	−6	350
73	800	33	640	−7	350
72	800	32	630	−8	340
71	800	31	620	−9	330
70	800	30	620	−10	330
69	800	29	610	−11	320
68	800	28	600	−12	310
67	800	27	600	−13	310
66	800	26	590	−14	300
65	800	25	580	−15	290
64	800	24	580	−16	290
63	800	23	570	−17	280
62	800	22	560	−18	270
61	800	21	560	−19	260
60	800	20	550		
59	800	19	540		
58	800	18	530		
57	790	17	530		
56	790	16	520		
55	780	15	510		
54	770	14	500		
53	770	13	500		
52	760	12	490		
51	750	11	480		
50	750	10	470		
49	740	9	470		
48	730	8	460		
47	730	7	450		
46	720	6	440		
45	710	5	440		
44	710	4	430		
43	700	3	420		
42	700	2	410		
41	690	1	410		
40	680	0	400		
39	680	−1	390		
38	670	−2	380		
37	660	−3	380		
36	660	−4	370		

How Did You Do on the Subject Test in Physics?

After you score your test and analyze your performance, think about the following questions:

Did you run out of time before reaching the end of the test?

If so, you may need to pace yourself better. For example, maybe you spent too much time on one or two hard questions. A better approach might be to skip the ones you can't answer right away and try answering all the questions that remain on the test. Then if there's time, go back to the questions you skipped.

Did you take a long time reading the directions?

You will save time when you take the test by learning the directions to the Subject Test in Physics ahead of time. Each minute you spend reading directions during the test is a minute that you could use to answer questions.

How did you handle questions you were unsure of?

If you were able to eliminate one or more of the answer choices as wrong and guess from the remaining ones, your approach probably worked to your advantage. On the other hand, making haphazard guesses or omitting questions without trying to eliminate choices could cost you valuable points.

How difficult were the questions for you compared with other students who took the test?

Table A shows you how difficult the multiple-choice questions were for the group of students who took this test during its national administration. The right-hand column gives the percentage of students that answered each question correctly.

A question answered correctly by almost everyone in the group is obviously an easier question. For example, 91 percent of the students answered question 6 correctly. But only 23 percent answered question 21 correctly.

Keep in mind that these percentages are based on just one group of students. They would probably be different with another group of students taking the test.

If you missed several easier questions, go back and try to find out why: Did the questions cover material you haven't yet reviewed? Did you misunderstand the directions?

Answer Explanations

For Practice Test 1

Question 1

Choice (A) is the correct answer. The gravitational potential energy is greatest at the highest point. The other four points are at a lower height.

Question 2

Choice (B) is the correct answer. The kinetic energy is greatest when the gravitational potential energy is lowest, which is at the lowest point. The other four points are at a higher height.

Question 3

Choice (A) is the correct answer. The ball in this option has the greatest initial horizontal velocity and thus travels the greatest horizontal distance. The ball in choices (B) and (C) have no horizontal velocity and will not travel horizontally. The ball in option (D) has a downward vertical velocity and thus will be in the air for less time than the ball in option (A), and also, its initial horizontal velocity is less than that of the ball in option (A), so the ball in option (D) will not travel as far horizontally.

Question 4

Choice (E) is the correct answer. Since all four are thrown with the same initial velocity, they all start with the same kinetic energy. Also, since they are all thrown from the same height, they all start with the same potential energy. Therefore, starting with the same mechanical energy and landing at the same height, they all land with the same kinetic energy and the same speed.

Question 5

Choice (E) is the correct answer. The gravitational field of Earth provides the only force acting on the ball in all four cases, so the acceleration is the same in all four cases.

Question 6

Choice (B) is the correct answer. The time of flight is determined by the vertical motion of the ball. Since the ball is thrown upward in (B), it will remain in flight for the longest duration in this case.

Question 7

Choice (B) is the correct answer. In a vacuum, all colors of light travel at the speed of light, but their wavelengths and frequencies are different.

Question 8

Choice (D) is the correct answer. As light passes from air into glass, the light slows down. Since every wave that strikes the glass from air creates a wave in the glass, the frequency of the waves does not change. Since the frequency stays the same and the wave slows down, the wavelength must change.

Question 9

Choice (B) is the correct answer. According to the equation for the restoring force of an "ideal" spring, $F = -kx$, the restoring force is directly proportional to the displacement of the block.

Question 10

Choice (E) is the correct answer. The elastic potential energy stored in the spring and the block's displacement from its equilibrium position follow a quadratic relationship according to the equation $U = \frac{1}{2}kx^2$, so the graph would be a parabola.

Question 11

Choice (E) is the correct answer. A force that is constant in magnitude and direction would create an acceleration that is also constant in magnitude and direction. Since acceleration is the slope of the velocity as a function of time, constant acceleration would create a straight line graph. Choice (E) is the only one that is not a straight line.

Question 12

Choice (D) is the correct answer. The direction of the velocity along a line is indicated by whether the sign has a positive or negative value. Since choice (D) is the only choice that changes sign between t = 0 and t = t_1, it is the only choice in which the velocity changes direction.

Question 13

Choice (A) is the correct answer. The net work done on the charge is directly proportional to the change in electrical potential between the two points. The electric potential around an isolated charge depends on the radial distance from it. For figures II and III, points X and Y are the same distance from the isolated charge and thus no work is done in moving the charge. Work is only done in figure I.

Question 14

Choice (D) is the correct answer. As noted in the prior explanation, no work is done in figures II and III.

Question 15

Choice (A) is the correct answer. Electrical potential is inversely proportional to the radial distance from the isolated charge. For figures II and III, points X and Y are the same distance from the isolated charge and thus are at the same electric potential. For figure I, point Y is closer to the isolated charge and thus is at a higher potential than point X.

Question 16

Choice (B) is the correct answer. That electrons are ejected from the surface of a metal upon absorbing enough energy from incident photons demonstrates the particle nature of light. The spectrum of a gas and an electron's diffraction pattern both demonstrate the wave nature of electrons.

Question 17

Choice (B) is the correct answer. Photons striking a metal surface require a threshold amount of energy in order to dislodge electrons from the surface of the material.

Question 18

Choice (B) is the correct answer. Convex mirrors can only create virtual images.

Question 19

Choice (E) is the correct answer. A converging lens makes a real, smaller image when the object is outside $2f$ from the lens; a real, larger image when the object is between $2f$ and f; and a virtual image when the object is inside of f.

Question 20

Choice (B) is the correct answer. The length of the string will determine the wavelength, so the wavelength stays the same. The thicker string will have a greater linear density, so the waves on this string will travel at a slower speed. For a given wavelength, a slower wave speed corresponds to a lower frequency.

Question 21

Choice (E) is the correct answer. Tightening the string on the guitar does not change the length, so the wavelength stays the same. The string will be under more tension (and it can be argued that the linear density will decrease because less mass will be present in the same length) and thus the wave will move faster. For a given wavelength, a faster wave speed corresponds to a higher frequency.

Question 22

Choice (E) is the correct answer. The coefficient of friction μ is the ratio of the frictional force to the normal force and thus has no units.

Question 23

Choice (D) is the correct answer. The change in speed can be determined by multiplying the acceleration by the time. So $\Delta v = at =$ $(20 \text{ m/s}^2)(3\text{s}) = 60 \text{ m/s}$.

Question 24

Choice (C) is the correct answer. Constant velocity occurs when the net force is zero. Since the surface is rough, there must be a frictional force present. Therefore, the friction and the tension must be equal in magnitude and opposite in direction to cancel out and make the net force zero.

Question 25

Choice (B) is the correct answer. The reading on the scale is the normal force, which is also the apparent weight of the box; it can be determined using the formula $F = m(g \pm a)$. When the elevator is accelerating upward, the plus sign is used. Thus, the normal force would be $F = (2 \text{ kg})(10 \text{ m/s}^2 + 2 \text{ m/s}^2) = 24 \text{ N}$.

Question 26

Choice (B) is the correct answer. Diffraction is a wave property, so this demonstrates that light can act as a wave.

Question 27

Choice (E) is the correct answer. The colors of a rainbow form as light enters water particles in the air, separates into its colors because each color refracts a different amount in the water and then reenters the air as a spectrum of colors. This is the same process seen in the spectrum created by a glass prism. Choices (A), (C), and (D) all create colors through interference patterns. Choice (B) creates colors through selective absorption or reflection of colors.

Question 28

Choice (D) is the correct answer. Since the graph has distance on the horizontal axis, it can be used to determine the wavelength of the wave. From the graph, the length of a single pulse is 5 m. The period can then be calculated using the equation for wave speed:

$$v = \lambda f = \frac{\lambda}{T} \therefore T = \frac{\lambda}{v} = \frac{(5 \text{ m})}{(2.0 \text{ m/s})} = 2.5 \text{ s}.$$

Question 29

Choice (B) is the correct answer. The astronaut's weight is the gravitational force between the astronaut and the planet. Using the equation $F = G\dfrac{m_1 m_2}{r^2}$, if one mass is doubled and everything else stays the same, the gravitational force (and the astronaut's weight) is doubled.

Question 30

Choice (A) is the correct answer. The average speed is the total distance traveled divided by the total time. The total distance can be determined by taking the area under the speed/time graph. The graph shown has two rectangles with a total area of $d_{tot} = Area = \ell_1 w_1 + \ell_2 w_2 = (6s)(2m/s) + (10s)(3m/s) = 42$ m. The average speed would then be

$$v = \frac{d_{tot}}{t_{tot}} = \frac{42 \text{ m}}{20 \text{ s}} = 2.1 \text{ m/s.}$$

Question 31

Choice (D) is the correct answer. For a velocity as a function of time graph, the object is at rest when the graph is at zero velocity, which is at the horizontal axis. This occurs for points B and E.

Question 32

Choice (D) is the correct answer. For a velocity as a function of time graph, the acceleration is the slope of the line. Since the slope is zero between points C and D, this is where the magnitude of the acceleration is at a minimum.

Question 33

Choice (B) is the correct answer. For a velocity as a function of time graph, the distance is the area under the curve. At point B, the distance would be the area of the triangle, $d = \frac{1}{2}bh = \frac{1}{2}(2t)(-2v) = -2vt$, with the negative sign representing the direction away from the starting point.

Traveling from point B to E, the object moves in the positive direction for a distance equal to the area of the trapezoid, $d = \frac{1}{2}(b_1 + b_1)$ $h = \frac{1}{2}(3t + t)(v) = 2vt$. So the total distance from the starting point to point E would be the two areas added together: $d = -2vt + 2vt = 0$. Thus, the object is the greatest distance from the starting position when it is at point B.

Question 34

Choice (C) is the correct answer. The equation for specific heat c is $Q = mc\Delta T$, where Q is the heat added or lost, m is the mass of the object, and ΔT is the change in temperature. Solving this for specific heat:

$$c = \frac{Q}{m\Delta T} = \frac{Q}{m(T_f - T_0)}.$$

Question 35

Choice (A) is the correct answer. The work done by the engine is the difference between the energy absorbed by the engine and the energy exhausted to the heat sink, or 600 J – 500 J = 100 J.

Question 36

Choice (D) is the correct answer. The power is the amount of work done in joules during each second. Since there are 20 cycles per second and X joules per cycle, the power can be calculated using the equation

$$P = \left(\frac{20 \text{ cycles}}{\text{second}}\right)\left(\frac{X \text{ joules}}{\text{cycles}}\right) = 20X \frac{\text{joules}}{\text{second}} = 20X \text{ watts}.$$

Question 37

Choice (B) is the correct answer. The ideal efficiency for a heat engine is given by the formula

$$eff = \frac{T_H - T_C}{T_H} \times 100\% = \frac{(360K - 270K)}{(360K)} \times 100\% = 25\%.$$

Question 38

Choice (D) is the correct answer. When the hot water is poured into the mug, the parts of the thermometer will expand as they heat up. The level of the liquid in the thermometer initially drops, indicating that the thermometer glass must have expanded first. After the glass heats up, the liquid will heat up and expand. Choice (A) might explain the observation, but it is incorrect because the liquid in the thermometer would never contract when the hot water is poured into the mug.

Question 39

Choice (B) is the correct answer. Since the hot water makes contact with the inner wall of the mug, the inner wall expands first, and if it expands too quickly, the mug can crack.

Question 40

Choice (A) is the correct answer. Isotopes have the same number of protons but a different number of neutrons. Therefore, they will have different atomic masses.

Question 41

Choice (D) is the correct answer. The theory of relativity states that all observers measure the speed of light as the same value, no matter the motion of the source or observer. So the speed of a laser light will always be measured as 3×10^8 m/s.

Question 42

Choice (C) is the correct answer. Protons and electrons have charges of different signs, have different masses, and are different sizes. Furthermore, electrons are leptons and are not made of quarks. There is currently no evidence that either a proton or an electron has decayed.

Question 43

Choice (C) is the correct answer. Since protons are the source of charge in the nucleus, two nuclei with the same charge will have the same number of protons. This also accounts for the positive charge of the nuclei. However, the nucleus contains most of the mass of the atom, so only I and II are correct.

Question 44

Choice (D) is the correct answer. When the uncharged ball is touched to the ball on the left, that ball loses charge. Since there is less charge, the force of repulsion is less. Since the force is less, the balls will hang at a lower angle. By Newton's third law, the balls still exert equal and opposite forces on each other, so the balls still hang at equal (but lower) angles.

Question 45

Choice (E) is the correct answer. Since the two particles reach the negative plate at the same time, they must have the same acceleration. In an electric field, the equation $F = qE$ shows that the force exerted on a particle is directly proportional to the charge on it. By Newton's second law, the acceleration of particle is directly proportional to the force on the particle and therefore directly proportional to the charge of the particle and is inversely proportional to the mass of the particle. So the two particles will reach the negative plate at the same time if they have the same charge-to-mass ratio.

Question 46

Choice (E) is the correct answer. The equation for the magnetic force on a current-carrying wire is $F_M = ILB\sin\theta$, where I is the current in the wire, L is the length of wire, B is the strength of the magnetic field, and θ is the angle between the magnetic field and the wire. Since the wire and field are perpendicular to each other, all three roman numerals (I, II, and III) are correct.

Question 47

Choice (A) is the correct answer. Connecting the inner compasses to each other would create a circle. Connecting the outer compasses to each other would create a larger circle. So the compasses create circles around point *P*, which is the shape of a magnetic field around a current-carrying wire passing perpendicularly through the table at point *P*.

Question 48

Choice (C) is the correct answer. Using the right-hand rule, if a positively charged particle is moving toward the left in a magnetic field directed out of the page, the magnetic force on the particle is directed toward the top of the page.

Question 49

Choice (B) is the correct answer. A transformer relies on the magnetic flux from a changing current in the primary coil to induce a voltage in the secondary coil. For choice (A), while a transformer has an iron core, it does not reduce magnetic flux. For options (C) and (D), a transformer is an AC device, but it is based on an inductor, not a resistor or capacitor. For option (E), a motor that is run backwards is a generator.

Question 50

Choice (A) is the correct answer. The equation for the induced electric potential difference is $\varepsilon = BLv\sin\theta$. Therefore, to create a potential difference, the length of the bar, the velocity of the bar, and the magnetic field must all be mutually perpendicular to each other. In choices (B), (C), and (D), the velocity and length are parallel. In choice (E), the magnetic field and length are parallel.

Question 51

Choice (B) is the correct answer. It takes Earth 365.25 days to go around the Sun, so it is not an integer multiple of the period of Earth's rotation on its axis.

Question 52

Choice (A) is the correct answer. Superconducting electromagnetics have almost zero electrical resistance and do not lose much electrical energy due to Joule heating. Thus, they use less electrical power compared to conventional electromagnets.

Question 53

Choice (C) is the correct answer. The stem graph shows that the wavelength is directly proportional to the period of the wave. Since the period is inversely proportional to the frequency of the wave, the wavelength is also inversely proportional to the frequency. This is shown in graph (C).

Question 54

Choice (A) is the correct answer. Different colors of light refract at different angles in a glass prism. This is because they travel at different speeds in the glass prism, and since each color has a different frequency, the speed of the light in the glass prism varies with frequency.

Question 55

Choice (A) is the correct answer. All parts of a converging lens converge the light for the image at the same point. Even if you cover up half the lens, the other half of the lens will still converge the remaining light at the same point. So, while the image would be less bright, the entire object would still be part of the image.

Question 56

Choice (D) is the correct answer. The period and frequency are related by the equation $T = \frac{1}{f}$.

Question 57

Choice (D) is the correct answer. First, capacitors C_2 and C_3 are combined in series using the equation $\frac{1}{C_S} = \frac{1}{C_1} + \frac{1}{C_2} = \frac{1}{8} + \frac{1}{8} = \frac{2}{8} \therefore C_S = 4\text{pF}$. Then that combination is combined in parallel with C_1 using the equation $C_{EQ} = C_1 + C_S = 4 + 4 = 8\text{pF}$.

Question 58

Choice (C) is the correct answer. The voltage between points A and B is the same as the voltage in the battery, which is 6 V. That is also the voltage across C_1. Since $C_2 = C_3$, the 6 V will split equally between them. So the voltage across both C_2 and C_3 is 3 V.

Question 59

Choice (A) is the correct answer. To confirm Ohm's law, the graph of potential difference and current should be a straight line. The ammeter and both resistors must be in series with the battery (choices A and C). The voltmeter must be in parallel to the fixed value resistor. If the potential difference is measured across the variable resistor (choice C), the graph would not be linear, so it would not be possible to confirm Ohm's law.

Question 60

Choice (A) is the correct answer. To confirm Ohm's law, the graph of potential difference as a function of current must be a straight line that goes through the origin.

Question 61

Choice (D) is the correct answer. The potential difference range is 9.5 to 10.5 volts. The resistance range is 1.5 to 2.5 amperes. Thus, the power ($P = VI$) range is 14.25 to 26.25, so the percentage is most nearly 30%.

Question 62

Choice (D) is the correct answer. Whether the spring is stretched or compressed, it will have elastic potential energy. Since the spring has mass, it will also have kinetic energy at all points when the speed is not zero (i.e., everywhere except the endpoints of oscillation).

Question 63

Choice (C) is the correct answer. When air resistance is a factor, the acceleration starts out as g and decreases as the ball picks up speed and the force of air resistance increases until terminal velocity is reached (at which point the acceleration becomes zero).

Question 64

Choice (A) is the correct answer. When the force of air resistance is equal to the force of gravity, the net force on the ball is zero. Thus, the acceleration is zero and the velocity is constant.

Question 65

Choice (B) is the correct answer. The law of conservation of momentum of a system states that the momentum of the system is conserved if the sum of the external forces exerted on the system is zero.

Question 66

Choice (D) is the correct answer. Using the formula for centripetal force,

$$F_c = \frac{mv^2}{r} = \frac{(4 \text{ kg})(2 \text{ m/s})^2}{20 \text{ m}} = 0.8 \text{ N.}$$

Question 67

Choice (B) is the correct answer. In an electron microscope, magnetic fields are used to control the motion of moving electrons and focus the beam.

Question 68

Choice (B) is the correct answer. In order to move forward, the person pushes back on the sled and (according to Newton's third law) the sled pushes forward on the person. Thus, the sled pushes the person toward the dock, and the person pushes the sled away from the dock.

Question 69

Choice (A) is the correct answer. In the frame of the person–sled system, there are no external forces, so the speed of the center of mass of the system must remain zero at all times. Therefore, if the person stops, the sled must also stop to keep the speed of the center of mass of the system zero.

Question 70

Choice (D) is the correct answer. Using conservation of momentum and the convention that velocity to the right is positive and to the left is negative, $m_1 v_{1i} + m_2 v_{2i} = m_1 v_{1f} + m_2 v_{2f}$ $\therefore$ $(0.2)(8) + (1)(2) = (0.2)(-2) + (1)v_{2f}$ $\therefore v_{2f} = 4.0$ m/s.

Question 71

Choice (E) is the correct answer. In order for the kinetic energy to not be changing, the speed of the object must remain constant. The force does not change the speed of the object if the force is perpendicular to the velocity. This is only true in choice (E).

Question 72

Choice (C) is the correct answer. The distance D and the time the ball is in the air will both increase if the vertical component of the initial velocity increases while the horizontal component stays the same or increases. Increasing θ_0 will decrease the horizontal component of the initial velocity if the angle is above 45°. So choices (A) and (D) will not always be true. Decreasing θ_0 will always decrease the vertical component of the initial velocity and thus decrease the time the ball is in the air. So choices (B) and (E) will never be true.

Question 73

Choice (B) is the correct answer. By knowing the diameter of the drum, the distance traveled by the beam of particles can be determined. By knowing the rotational speed of the drum and the angle from the slit, the time it takes the target to move to a position directly across from the beam can be determined. Using the ratio of distance over time, the speed of the particle can be determined.

Question 74

Choice (E) is the correct answer. Acceleration due to gravity on a planet can be determined using Newton's law of universal gravitation:

$$mg = G\frac{Mm}{R^2} \therefore g = \frac{GM}{R^2}.$$

So, for Planet X,

$$a_X = \frac{GM}{R_X^2}. \text{ For planet } Y, a_Y = \frac{GM}{(3R_X)^2} = \frac{1}{9}\frac{GM}{R_X^2} = \frac{a_X}{9}.$$

Question 75

Choice (E) is the correct answer. Since the car is moving with constant velocity, the net force must be zero and therefore has no direction associated with it.

Physics Subject Test - Practice Test 2

Practice Helps

The test that follows is an actual, previously administered SAT Subject Test in Physics. To get an idea of what it's like to take this test, practice under conditions that are much like those of an actual test administration.

- Set aside an hour when you can take the test uninterrupted.

- Sit at a desk or table with no other books or papers. Dictionaries, other books, or notes are not allowed in the test room.

- Do not use a calculator. Calculators are not allowed for the Subject Test in Physics.

- Tear out an answer sheet from the back of this book and fill it in just as you would on the day of the test. One answer sheet can be used for up to three Subject Tests.

- Read the instructions that precede the practice test. During the actual administration, you will be asked to read them before answering test questions.

- Time yourself by placing a clock or kitchen timer in front of you.

- After you finish the practice test, read the sections "How to Score the SAT Subject Test in Physics" and "How Did You Do on the Subject Test in Physics?"

- The appearance of the answer sheet in this book may differ from the answer sheet you see on test day.

PHYSICS TEST

The top portion of the page of the answer sheet that you will use in taking the Physics Test must be filled in exactly as illustrated below. When your supervisor tells you to fill in the circle next to the name of the test you are about to take, mark your answer sheet as shown.

○ Literature	○ Mathematics Level 1	○ German	○ Chinese Listening	○ Japanese Listening
○ Biology E	○ Mathematics Level 2	○ Italian	○ French Listening	○ Korean Listening
○ Biology M	○ U.S. History	○ Latin	○ German Listening	○ Spanish Listening
○ Chemistry	○ World History	○ Modern Hebrew		
● Physics	○ French	○ Spanish	**Background Questions:** ① ② ③ ④ ⑤ ⑥ ⑦ ⑧ ⑨	

After filling in the circle next to the name of the test you are taking, locate the Background Questions section, which also appears at the top of your answer sheet (as shown above). This is where you will answer the following Background Questions on your answer sheet.

BACKGROUND QUESTIONS

Please answer the three questions below by filling in the appropriate circle in the Background Questions box on your answer sheet. The information you provide is for statistical purposes only and will not affect your test score.

Question 1

How many semesters of physics have you taken in high school, including any semester in which you are currently enrolled? (Count as two semesters any case in which a full year's course is taught in a one-semester [half-year] compressed schedule.) Fill in only one circle of circles 1-3.

- One semester or less —Fill in circle 1.
- Two semesters —Fill in circle 2.
- Three semesters or more —Fill in circle 3.

Question 2

About how often did you do lab work in your first physics course? (Include any times when you may have watched a film or a demonstration by your teacher and then discussed or analyzed data.) Fill in only one circle of circles 4-7.

- Less than once a week —Fill in circle 4.
- About once a week —Fill in circle 5.
- A few times a week —Fill in circle 6.
- Almost every day —Fill in circle 7.

Question 3

If you have taken or are currently taking an Advanced Placement (AP) Physics course, which of the following describes the course? Fill in both circles if applicable. (If you have never had AP Physics, leave circles 8 and 9 blank.)

- A course that uses algebra and trigonometry
  but NOT calculus (Physics 1 and/or Physics 2) —Fill in circle 8.
- A course that uses calculus (Physics C) —Fill in circle 9.

When the supervisor gives the signal, turn the page and begin the Physics Test. There are 100 numbered circles on the answer sheet and 75 questions in the Physics Test. Therefore, use only circles 1 to 75 for recording your answers.

PHYSICS TEST

Note: To simplify calculations, you may use $g = 10$ m/s^2 for the acceleration due to gravity at Earth's surface.

Part A

Directions: Each set of lettered choices below refers to the numbered questions immediately following it. Select the one lettered choice that best answers each question, and then fill in the corresponding circle on the answer sheet. A choice may be used once, more than once, or not at all in each set.

Questions 1-3

The graph below shows the temperature of a sample of pure water as a function of the energy added to the sample. The water is initially ice and is then taken through the liquid and gaseous phases.

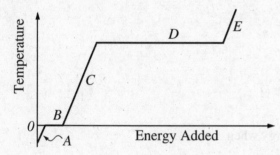

1. Portion of the graph corresponding to the water boiling

2. Portion of the graph corresponding to the liquid water getting warmer

3. Portion of the graph corresponding to the ice melting

Questions 4-5

An ideal gas undergoes a process from an initial state to a final state. The process may be one of the following.

(A) A constant-temperature process

(B) A constant-volume process

(C) A constant-pressure process

(D) A process by which pressure, volume, and temperature all increase

(E) A process by which pressure, volume, and temperature all decrease

4. For which process will the average kinetic energy of the molecules be constant throughout the entire process?

5. For which process will no work be done on or by the gas throughout the entire process?

GO ON TO THE NEXT PAGE

Questions 6-7

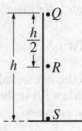

A stone is dropped from the top of the cliff of height h shown above. The stone is at point Q just after release. Point S is just above the ground. Let the gravitational potential energy be defined to be zero at the ground, and assume air resistance is negligible.

(A) It is 4 times that at R.

(B) It is 2 times that at R.

(C) It is $\sqrt{2}$ times that at R.

(D) It is the same as at R.

(E) It is half that at R.

6. How does the acceleration of the stone at Q compare to that at R ?

7. How does the gravitational potential energy when the stone is at Q compare to that at R ?

Questions 8-10

The table below includes three properties of the net force on an object: the magnitude, direction, and angle with respect to the object's path. For each situation in the questions that follow, select the choice that indicates whether these quantities are constant or changing during the course of the motion.

	Magnitude of Net Force	Direction of Net Force	Angle of Net Force with Respect to Path
(A)	Constant	Constant	Constant
(B)	Constant	Constant	Changing
(C)	Constant	Changing	Constant
(D)	Changing	Constant	Constant
(E)	Changing	Changing	Constant

8. A block sliding down a frictionless inclined plane

9. A satellite moving in a circular orbit at constant speed

10. A projectile following a parabolic trajectory near Earth's surface

GO ON TO THE NEXT PAGE

Questions 11-12 refer to the following types of energy.

(A) Gravitational potential energy
(B) Electrical potential energy
(C) Elastic potential energy
(D) Nuclear potential energy
(E) Kinetic energy

11. The energy that increases as a simple pendulum swings upward toward the highest point of its swing

12. The major source of the energy released by a uranium atom undergoing fission

Questions 13-14 refer to the following types of spectra.

I. Continuous spectrum
II. Bright-line spectrum
III. Dark-line spectrum

(A) I only
(B) II only
(C) III only
(D) II and III only
(E) I, II, and III

13. Which of these spectra does a glowing light bulb filament produce?

14. Which of these spectra does the gas discharge tube of a neon sign produce?

Questions 15-16

The following are positions at which electric or magnetic fields may exist. Assume that in each position there are no electric or magnetic fields other than those due to the charges or currents mentioned.

(A) Inside a charged hollow metal sphere
(B) In the vicinity of a bar magnet
(C) In the vicinity of an electric point charge
(D) Midway between two infinitely long and wide parallel plates carrying charges of equal magnitude and the same sign
(E) Midway between two infinitely long parallel wires carrying equal currents in the same direction

15. Where must there exist an electric field that is <u>not</u> equal to zero?

16. Where must there exist a magnetic field that is <u>not</u> equal to zero?

GO ON TO THE NEXT PAGE

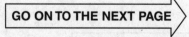

Questions 17-18 refer to the following possible directions for magnetic fields or forces.

(A) Toward the left
(B) Toward the right
(C) Toward the bottom of the page
(D) Toward the top of the page
(E) Out of the page

Current

17. A wire loop in the plane of the page carries a counterclockwise current, as shown above. What is the direction of the magnetic field at the center of the loop?

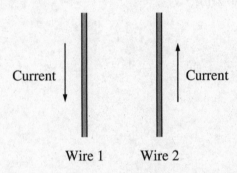

Current   Current

Wire 1   Wire 2

18. Wires 1 and 2 lie in the plane of the page and carry currents in opposite directions, as shown above. What is the direction of the magnetic force on wire 2 due to wire 1 ?

Questions 19-20

Each of the following pairs of electric charges is the same distance apart. Point P is equidistant from the charges in each case. Assume that each pair is isolated from all other charges.

(A) $+Q$ P $+Q$

(B) $+Q$ P $-Q$

(C) $+2Q$ P $-2Q$

(D) $-Q$ P $+2Q$

(E) $+2Q$ P $-Q$

19. For which pair is the electric field at P equal to zero?

20. For which pair is the magnitude of the electric field at P the greatest?

Questions 21-22

(A) Loudness
(B) Pitch
(C) Quality (timbre)
(D) Beats
(E) Resonance

21. Primarily determined by the amplitude of a sound wave

22. For a vibrating string of fixed length, always increases with an increase in tension

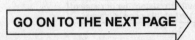GO ON TO THE NEXT PAGE

Part B

Directions: Each of the questions or incomplete statements below is followed by five suggested answers or completions. Select the one that is best in each case and then fill in the corresponding circle on the answer sheet.

23. A block of weight W is moving to the right, pushed across a floor by horizontal force P. The force due to friction is f, and the normal force is N. Which of the following diagrams best shows the forces acting on the block?

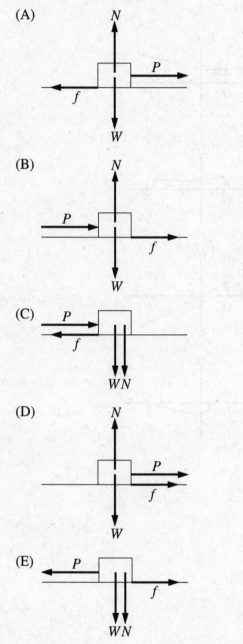

(A)

(B)

(C)

(D)

(E)

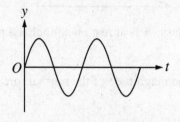

24. The vertical displacement y of a ball is given as a function of time t in the graph above. The motion of which of the following balls could have created the graph?

    I. Ball I is in free fall under the influence of a constant gravitational force.
    II. Ball II is floating in a ripple tank.
    III. Ball III is attached to the end of a vertical spring.

(A) I only
(B) III only
(C) I and II only
(D) II and III only
(E) I, II, and III

25. On a trip to Washington, D.C., a group of students ran up the steps of the Capitol building. If they all started together and stopped at the top at the same time, which of the students expended the greatest average power in overcoming gravity to make the climb?

(A) The heaviest
(B) The lightest
(C) They all expended the same average nonzero power.
(D) None of them expended power, since energy is always conserved.
(E) It cannot be determined without knowing the total mass of all the students.

Questions 26-27

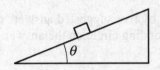

A box of mass m is at rest on an inclined plane, as shown above.

26. What is the magnitude of the normal force on the box?

(A) Zero
(B) mg
(C) $mg\ \tan\theta$
(D) $mg\ \sin\theta$
(E) $mg\ \cos\theta$

27. What is the direction of the net force on the box?

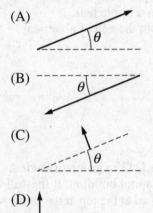

(E) The net force has no direction because it is zero.

28. The following diagrams show the path of a light ray from an object O passing through a thin lens having focal points F. Which ray diagram CANNOT be correct for either a converging or a diverging lens?

(A)
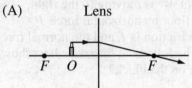

(B)
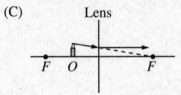

(C)
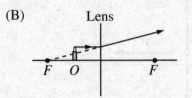

(D)
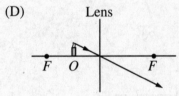

(E)
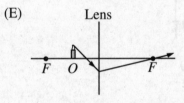

29. Which of the following is a phenomenon that is observed for light waves in air but <u>not</u> for sound waves in air?

    (A) Polarization
    (B) Interference
    (C) Diffraction
    (D) Attenuation
    (E) Resonance

30. When monochromatic light is passed through two narrow parallel slits, processes that occur include which of the following?

    I. The light is diffracted at each slit.
    II. The waves from the two slits exhibit interference.
    III. The wavelength of the light decreases.

    (A) I only
    (B) III only
    (C) I and II only
    (D) II and III only
    (E) I, II, and III

31. If a satellite in a circular orbit moves with constant speed, then its

    (A) momentum changes in direction
    (B) potential energy changes in magnitude
    (C) potential energy changes in direction
    (D) kinetic energy changes in direction
    (E) centripetal and tangential accelerations are both zero

32. Ball 1 is thrown straight down from the top of a building with a given initial speed. At the same time ball 2 is thrown straight up from the top of the same building with the same initial speed. Air resistance is negligible. If ball 1 has a speed v just before hitting the ground, what is the speed of ball 2 just before hitting the ground?

    (A) $4v$
    (B) $2v$
    (C) v
    (D) $v/2$
    (E) $v/4$

33. An object with zero acceleration will

    (A) move along the trajectory of a projectile
    (B) change speed without changing direction
    (C) change direction without changing speed
    (D) maintain constant circular motion
    (E) maintain constant speed and direction

34. A student decides to investigate the electrical shock she receives as she gets out of her car. Which of the following factors is LEAST likely to have a significant effect on the size of the shock?

    (A) The materials her clothing contains
    (B) The distance she slides across the seat when getting out
    (C) The part of the car she touches as she gets out
    (D) The humidity of the air
    (E) Whether the engine is running

GO ON TO THE NEXT PAGE

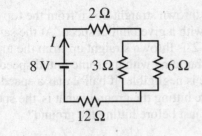

35. Four resistors are connected in a circuit with a power supply, as shown in the figure above. A current *I* leaves the battery. Which resistor in the circuit dissipates the most power?

(A) The 2 Ω resistor
(B) The 3 Ω resistor
(C) The 6 Ω resistor
(D) The 12 Ω resistor
(E) All four resistors dissipate the same power.

36. You are given only a coil of wire, a battery of unknown emf, and connecting wires and are asked to determine the resistance of the coil. Which of the following additional instruments should you request?

   I. A voltmeter
  II. An ammeter
 III. An electroscope

(A) I only
(B) II only
(C) III only
(D) I and II only
(E) II and III only

GO ON TO THE NEXT PAGE

Questions 37-39

The graph below shows the displacement of a mouse running in a straight, narrow, 8-meter-long tunnel. The entrance of the tunnel is taken as the origin.

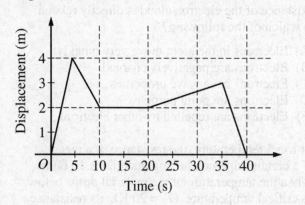

37. What is the farthest position the mouse reaches inside the tunnel?

(A) 3 meters into the tunnel
(B) 4 meters into the tunnel
(C) 7 meters into the tunnel
(D) The end of the tunnel
(E) It cannot be determined from the information given.

38. What is the average speed of the mouse for the interval from 10 to 35 seconds?

(A) 0 m/s

(B) $\frac{1}{25}$ m/s

(C) $\frac{1}{15}$ m/s

(D) $\frac{3}{25}$ m/s

(E) $\frac{1}{5}$ m/s

39. What is the magnitude of the average velocity of the mouse for the 40-second interval?

(A) 0 m/s

(B) $\frac{1}{10}$ m/s

(C) $\frac{1}{5}$ m/s

(D) $\frac{1}{4}$ m/s

(E) $\frac{2}{5}$ m/s

GO ON TO THE NEXT PAGE

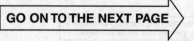

40. A diver is lying at the bottom of a calm pool of water. A bird is in a tree above the water, directly over the diver's feet. Correct statements about this situation include which of the following?

   I. To the diver, the bird will appear to be higher above the ground than it actually is.
   II. To the diver, the bird and the tree will be inverted because the surface of the pool behaves like a lens.
   III. The bird cannot see the diver because the light is totally reflected by the surface of the water.

   (A) I only
   (B) III only
   (C) I and II only
   (D) II and III only
   (E) I, II, and III

41. A beam of light has a wavelength λ in air. If the beam passes from air into water, which has an index of refraction of $4/3$, its wavelength in the water is

   (A) $\dfrac{\lambda}{4}$

   (B) $\dfrac{3\lambda}{4}$

   (C) λ

   (D) 3λ

   (E) 4λ

42. According to the conservation of charge principle, which of the following is certain to be true when charged objects interact?

   (A) The charge on each object remains the same.
   (B) The number of charged objects is the same before and after the interaction.
   (C) The total net charge of the objects is the same before and after the interaction.
   (D) The total net charge of all the objects can change during the interaction only by an amount equal to an integer times the charge of an electron.
   (E) The total net charge of the objects can increase only if, in a later interaction, the total net charge decreases by an equal amount.

43. The present theory of matter postulates that electrons in an atom do not have fixed orbital radii. For each possible electron energy state, there are regions around the nucleus where there is a high probability of finding the electron, sometimes referred to as the electron cloud. The existence of the electron cloud is directly related to which of the following?

   (A) Electrons in the atom move very quickly.
   (B) Electrons are negatively charged.
   (C) Electrons have wave properties.
   (D) Electrons are point particles.
   (E) Electrons are repelled by other electrons.

44. At room temperature, the resistance of a piece of a certain superconducting material is 10 ohms. When the temperature of the material drops below its critical temperature $(T_c = 20 \text{ K})$, its resistance becomes

   (A) zero
   (B) $0.5 \ \Omega$
   (C) $2 \ \Omega$
   (D) $10 \ \Omega$
   (E) infinite

45. Of the following, which is the best estimate of the angular velocity of Earth's rotation?

   (A) 10^{-1} rev/s
   (B) 10^{-3} rev/s
   (C) 10^{-5} rev/s
   (D) 10^{-7} rev/s
   (E) 10^{-9} rev/s

46. The resistances of two resistors are measured to be 5.2 ± 0.3 ohms and 7.7 ± 0.2 ohms. These measurements are used to determine the net resistance when the resistors are placed in series. The error in the calculated value is most nearly

   (A) $\pm 0.06 \ \Omega$
   (B) $\pm 0.1 \ \Omega$
   (C) $\pm 0.5 \ \Omega$
   (D) $\pm 1.0 \ \Omega$
   (E) $\pm 2.5 \ \Omega$

GO ON TO THE NEXT PAGE

47. Which of the following is a correct evaluation

   of the expression $\dfrac{(2 \text{ kg})(2 \text{ m/s}^2)(2 \text{ m})}{2 \text{ s}}$?

   (A) 4 kg·m/s
   (B) 4 N
   (C) 4 N·s
   (D) 4 J
   (E) 4 W

48. Experimental evidence of the existence of the top
   quark is considered to be essential in support of
   which of the following?

   (A) The standard model of particles and fields
   (B) The model of high-temperature
        superconductivity
   (C) The general theory of relativity
   (D) The special theory of relativity
   (E) The Bohr model of the atom

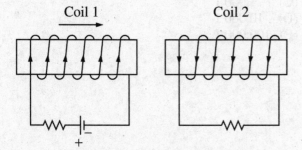

49. In the figure above, coil 1 is moving toward
   coil 2. Which of the following changes will
   increase the induced current in coil 2 ?

   I. The speed of coil 1 is increased.
   II. The number of turns in coil 1 is increased.
   III. The battery attached to coil 1 is replaced
        by one of higher emf.

   (A) I only
   (B) III only
   (C) I and II only
   (D) II and III only
   (E) I, II, and III

50. Two point charges are a distance r apart.
   Which of the following best shows the magnitude
   F of the electric force on either charge as a
   function of r ?

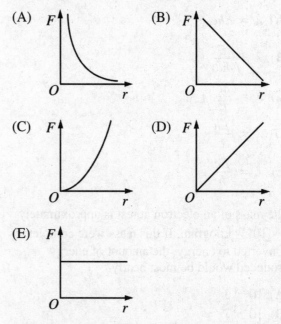

51. Two spheres, X and Y, are 8 meters apart. The
   charge on sphere X is 2 microcoulombs and the
   charge on sphere Y is 1 microcoulomb. If F is
   the magnitude of the force of X on Y, then what
   is the magnitude of the force of Y on X ?

   (A) $\dfrac{1}{8}F$

   (B) $\dfrac{1}{2}F$

   (C) F

   (D) $2F$

   (E) $8F$

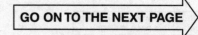

52. If the energy of a photon is E, which of the following is the correct expression for the wavelength λ of the photon in terms of its energy E, Planck's constant h, and the speed of light c ?

    (A) $\lambda = Ehc$

    (B) $\lambda = \dfrac{E}{hc}$

    (C) $\lambda = \dfrac{hc}{E}$

    (D) $\lambda = \dfrac{Eh}{c}$

    (E) $\lambda = \dfrac{Ec}{h}$

53. The mass of an electron at rest is approximately 9×10^{-31} kilogram. If this mass were completely converted to energy, the amount of energy produced would be most nearly

    (A) 10^{-21} J
    (B) 10^{-13} J
    (C) 10^{-8} J
    (D) 10^{-3} J
    (E) 10^{2} J

54. Assume that Earth is uniform in density. If Earth's radius could be doubled with its mass remaining the same, the magnitude of the gravitational acceleration on Earth's surface would be

    (A) $g/4$
    (B) $g/2$
    (C) g
    (D) $2g$
    (E) $4g$

55. A ball undergoes uniform circular motion with centripetal acceleration a. If both the radius of the circle and the speed of the ball are tripled, which of the following is the new acceleration of the ball?

    (A) $\dfrac{a}{9}$

    (B) $\dfrac{a}{3}$

    (C) $\dfrac{a}{\sqrt{3}}$

    (D) $3a$

    (E) $9a$

56. A 10-kilogram steel ball is dropped from the top of a tower 100 meters high. The kinetic energy of the ball just before it strikes the ground is most nearly

    (A)   10 J
    (B)   100 J
    (C)   1,000 J
    (D)   10,000 J
    (E) 100,000 J

GO ON TO THE NEXT PAGE
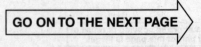

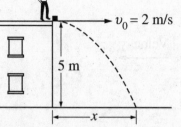

Note: Figure not drawn to scale.

57. A worker accidentally kicks a scrap of lumber off the flat roof of a building, giving it an initial horizontal speed v_0 of 2 meters per second. The building is 5 meters high, as shown above. If air resistance is negligible, the distance x from the edge of the building to where the wood scrap lands is most nearly

(A) 0.5 m
(B) 1.0 m
(C) 2.0 m
(D) 5.0 m
(E) 10 m

58. A projectile is fired from ground level at an angle of 60°. Air resistance is negligible. Which of the following is true of the projectile's velocity and acceleration vectors at the highest point of its path?

	Velocity Vector	Acceleration Vector
(A)	Equals zero	Equals zero
(B)	Equals zero	Points down
(C)	Points horizontally	Equals zero
(D)	Points horizontally	Points down
(E)	Points vertically	Points down

59. Which of the following is a completely inelastic collision?

(A) A ball rebounds against a wall, reversing its velocity.
(B) Two balls collide head on, each reversing its velocity.
(C) Two balls collide, stick to each other, and move together after the collision.
(D) Two balls collide and move at a right angle to each other after the collision.
(E) A ball with velocity **v** collides with a ball at rest; after the collision the first ball is at rest and the second ball has velocity **v**.

60. A toy truck of mass 0.6 kilogram initially coasts horizontally at a constant speed of 2 meters per second. A child drops a beanbag of mass 0.2 kilogram straight down into the truck. Immediately afterward, the speed of the truck is most nearly

(A) 0.3 m/s
(B) 1.2 m/s
(C) 1.5 m/s
(D) 2.0 m/s
(E) 2.4 m/s

61. A car moves along a straight road at constant speed until its brakes are applied. The car then slows down until it comes to a stop. Three quantities are measured: the car's mass, the speed of the car just before the brakes are applied, and the time it takes for the car to come to a stop. Which of the following can be calculated from this information?

  I. The average acceleration of the car
  II. The average net force exerted on the car
  III. The average power expended while the brakes are applied

(A) I only
(B) II only
(C) III only
(D) I and II only
(E) I, II, and III

Questions 62-63

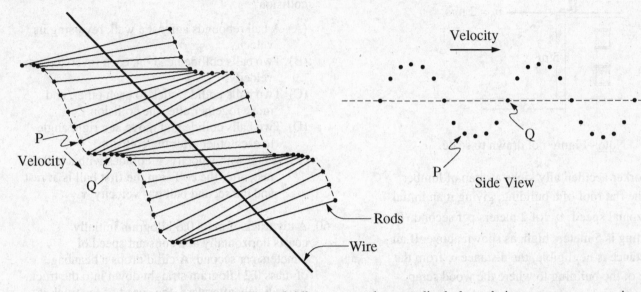

Velocity

Side View

Rods

Wire

A wave machine consists of many long rods rigidly connected perpendicularly at their centers to a taut wire. A wave generator moves one end of the last rod up and down, which causes a transverse wave with velocity **v** to travel on the machine, as shown above on the left. When the wave is traveling, the rod ends outline a sine wave. The side view, above on the right, shows the positions of the rod ends at a particular instant.

62. The wave generator suddenly increases the amplitude of the waves it is producing, but the frequency of the waves remains the same. Which of the following properties of the waves will also increase as a result?

   I. The average speed at which the rod ends move up and down

   II. The speed at which the wave moves along the rods

   III. The wavelength of the waves

(A) I only
(B) III only
(C) I and II only
(D) II and III only
(E) I, II, and III

63. Which of the following correctly describes the direction of motion of rod ends P and Q at the instant shown?

Rod End P	Rod End Q
(A) Up	Down
(B) Right	Left
(C) Right	Right
(D) Down	Down
(E) Up	At rest

GO ON TO THE NEXT PAGE

64. A siren on a fire truck creates a sound of frequency f when the truck is at rest. Which of the following correctly explains why the frequency of the siren heard by a stationary observer is higher than f when the truck is moving toward the observer?

   (A) The velocity of the waves is equal to the velocity of sound in air plus the truck's velocity.
   (B) The motion of the truck causes a decrease in the wavelength of waves reaching the observer.
   (C) The motion of the truck causes an increase in the amplitude of waves reaching the observer.
   (D) Different parts of the sound wave interfere because one part moves faster than the other.
   (E) The siren creates a higher frequency sound when the truck is moving.

65. Which of the following is true of sound waves?

   I. They carry energy.
   II. They carry momentum.
   III. They exert pressure.

   (A) None
   (B) I only
   (C) II only
   (D) III only
   (E) I, II, and III

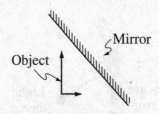

66. The diagram above is a top view of an object and a plane mirror. The image would appear to be in which of the following positions?

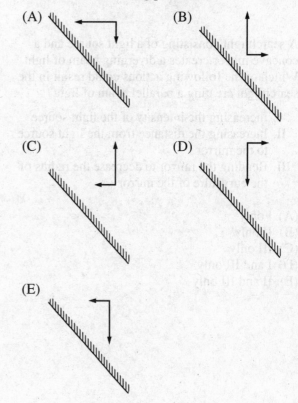

GO ON TO THE NEXT PAGE

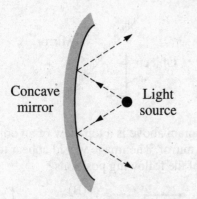

Concave mirror   Light source

67. A searchlight consisting of a light source and a concave mirror creates a diverging beam of light. Which of the following actions could result in the searchlight creating a parallel beam of light?

   I. Increasing the intensity of the light source
   II. Increasing the distance from the light source to the mirror
   III. Bending the mirror to decrease the radius of the curvature of the mirror

   (A) I only
   (B) II only
   (C) III only
   (D) I and III only
   (E) II and III only

68. A 2-kilogram toy car is traveling forward at 1 meter per second when it is hit in the rear by a 3-kilogram toy truck that was traveling at 3 meters per second just before impact. If the two toys stick together, their speed immediately after the collision is

   (A) 0.8 m/s
   (B) 1.4 m/s
   (C) 1.8 m/s
   (D) 2.0 m/s
   (E) 2.2 m/s

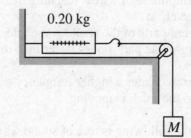

0.20 kg

M

69. A spring scale with a mass of 0.20 kilogram is attached at one end to a wall, as shown above. The other end of the scale is attached to a block of mass M by a string that passes over a frictionless pulley, so that the block hangs freely. The spring scale registers 10 newtons. The mass M of the block is most nearly

   (A) 0.8 kg
   (B) 1.0 kg
   (C) 1.2 kg
   (D) 1.5 kg
   (E) 2.0 kg

GO ON TO THE NEXT PAGE

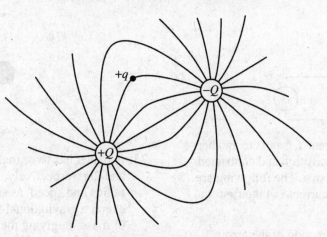

70. A small electric test charge $+q$ is placed as shown above in the electric field of a positive charge $+Q$ and a negative charge $-Q$. Which of the following best shows the direction of the net electric force on the charge $+q$?

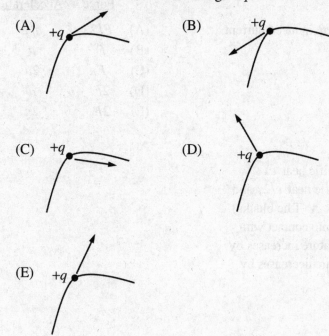

(A)

(B)

(C)

(D)

(E)

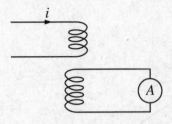

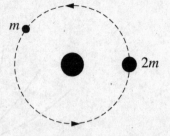

71. A coil of wire carrying current i is next to another coil of wire that is fixed in position and connected to an ammeter, as shown above. The following are four possible states for the current i in the first coil.

   I. Constant and in the direction of the arrow
  II. Constant and opposite to the direction of the arrow
  III. Increasing and in the direction of the arrow
  IV. Increasing and opposite to the direction of the arrow

Which of the states will create an induced current in the ammeter?

(A) I and II only
(B) I and III only
(C) II and IV only
(D) III and IV only
(E) I, II, III, and IV

72. Block A has mass M and specific heat c. Block B has mass $M/2$, specific heat $c/2$, and a higher temperature than block A. The blocks are thermally isolated and put into contact with each other. If block A's temperature increases by 20 K, then block B's temperature decreases by

(A)   5 K
(B) 10 K
(C) 20 K
(D) 40 K
(E) 80 K

73. A planet has two small satellites of mass m and $2m$, respectively, with the same orbital radius and speed, as shown above. The planet exerts a gravitational force F on the satellite of mass m, giving the satellite an acceleration of magnitude a. What gravitational force does the planet exert on the satellite of mass $2m$ and what is the magnitude of this satellite's resulting acceleration?

	Force	Acceleration
(A)	$F/2$	$a/2$
(B)	F	a
(C)	F	$2a$
(D)	$2F$	a
(E)	$2F$	$2a$

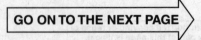

74. A ball is thrown at an angle of 30° above the horizontal, and air resistance is negligible. Under these conditions, each of the following statements concerning the ball at the highest point of its trajectory is true EXCEPT:

(A) Its kinetic energy is zero.
(B) Its acceleration is downward.
(C) Its velocity is horizontal.
(D) Its momentum is changing.
(E) Its gravitational potential energy is greater than at any other point in the trajectory.

75. In lifting off against Earth's gravity, the seat of a space shuttle exerts a vertical force of $4Mg$ on an astronaut of mass M. What is the astronaut's acceleration?

(A) $5g$
(B) $4g$
(C) $3g$
(D) $2g$
(E) g

STOP

IF YOU FINISH BEFORE TIME IS CALLED, YOU MAY CHECK YOUR WORK ON THIS TEST ONLY. DO NOT TURN TO ANY OTHER TEST IN THIS BOOK.

How to Score the SAT Subject Test in Physics

When you take an actual SAT Subject Test in Physics, your answer sheet will be "read" by a scanning machine that will record your response to each question. Then a computer will compare your answers with the correct answers and produce your raw score. You get one point for each correct answer. For each wrong answer, you lose one-fourth of a point. Questions you omit (and any for which you mark more than one answer) are not counted. This raw score is converted to a scaled score that is reported to you and to the colleges you specify.

Worksheet 1. Finding Your Raw Test Score

STEP 1: Table A on the following page lists the correct answers for all the questions on the Subject Test in Physics that is reproduced in this book. It also serves as a worksheet for you to calculate your raw score.

- Compare your answers with those given in the table.

- Put a check in the column marked "Right" if your answer is correct.

- Put a check in the column marked "Wrong" if your answer is incorrect.

- Leave both columns blank if you omitted the question.

STEP 2: Count the number of right answers.

Enter the total here: _____

STEP 3: Count the number of wrong answers.

Enter the total here: _____

STEP 4: Multiply the number of wrong answers by .250.

Enter the product here: _____

STEP 5: Subtract the result obtained in Step 4 from the total you obtained in Step 2.

Enter the result here: _____

STEP 6: Round the number obtained in Step 5 to the nearest whole number.

Enter the result here: _____

The number you obtained in Step 6 is your raw score.

Answers to Practice Test 2

Table A
Answers to the Subject Test in Physics - Practice Test 2 and Percentage of Students Answering Each Question Correctly

Question Number	Correct Answer	Right	Wrong	Percent Answering Correctly*	Question Number	Correct Answer	Right	Wrong	Percent Answering Correctly*
1	D			80	26	E			62
2	C			86	27	E			64
3	B			73	28	E			39
4	A			67	29	A			62
5	B			33	30	C			60
6	D			78	31	A			50
7	B			68	32	C			60
8	A			74	33	E			86
9	C			64	34	E			50
10	B			42	35	D			61
11	A			83	36	D			74
12	D			90	37	B			85
13	A			36	38	B			62
14	B			21	39	A			61
15	C			51	40	A			58
16	B			57	41	B			62
17	E			66	42	C			67
18	B			32	43	C			25
19	A			71	44	A			45
20	C			70	45	C			31
21	A			72	46	C			64
22	B			54	47	E			52
23	A			87	48	A			22
24	D			67	49	E			39
25	A			79	50	A			64

Table A continued on next page

Table A continued from previous page

Question Number	Correct Answer	Right	Wrong	Percent Answering Correctly*	Question Number	Correct Answer	Right	Wrong	Percent Answering Correctly*
51	C			50	66	A			48
52	C			42	67	E			37
53	B			38	68	E			58
54	A			57	69	B			51
55	D			60	70	A			40
56	D			70	71	D			25
57	C			51	72	E			36
58	D			53	73	D			51
59	C			64	74	A			44
60	C			51	75	C			30
61	E			57					
62	A			34					
63	A			26					
64	B			33					
65	E			34					

* These percentages are based on an analysis of the answer sheets for a random sample of 8,068 students who took the original administration of this test and whose mean score was 647. They may be used as an indication of the relative difficulty of a particular question. Each percentage may also be used to predict the likelihood that a typical Subject Test in Physics candidate will answer correctly that question on this edition of this test.

Note: Answer explanations can be found on page 112.

Finding Your Scaled Score

When you take SAT Subject Tests, the scores sent to the colleges you specify are reported on the College Board scale, which ranges from 200 to 800. You can convert your practice test score to a scaled score by using Table B. To find your scaled score, locate your raw score in the left-hand column of Table B; the corresponding score in the right-hand column is your scaled score. For example, a raw score of 38 on this particular edition of the Subject Test in Physics corresponds to a scaled score of 670.

Raw scores are converted to scaled scores to ensure that a score earned on any one edition of a particular Subject Test is comparable to the same scaled score earned on any other edition of the same Subject Test. Because some editions of the tests may be slightly easier or more difficult than others, College Board scaled scores are adjusted so that they indicate the same level of performance regardless of the edition of the test taken and the ability of the group that takes it. Thus, for example, a score of 400 on one edition of a test taken at a particular administration indicates the same level of achievement as a score of 400 on a different edition of the test taken at a different administration.

When you take the SAT Subject Tests during a national administration, your scores are likely to differ somewhat from the scores you obtain on the tests in this book. People perform at different levels at different times for reasons unrelated to the tests themselves. The precision of any test is also limited because it represents only a sample of all the possible questions that could be asked.

Table B
Scaled Score Conversion Table
Subject Test in Physics - Practice Test 2

Raw Score	Scaled Score	Raw Score	Scaled Score	Raw Score	Scaled Score
75	800	35	650	−5	370
74	800	34	650	−6	360
73	800	33	640	−7	360
72	800	32	630	−8	350
71	800	31	630	−9	340
70	800	30	620	−10	340
69	800	29	610	−11	330
68	800	28	610	−12	320
67	800	27	600	−13	310
66	800	26	590	−14	310
65	800	25	580	−15	300
64	800	24	580	−16	290
63	800	23	570	−17	280
62	800	22	560	−18	280
61	800	21	560	−19	270
60	800	20	550		
59	800	19	540		
58	790	18	530		
57	790	17	530		
56	780	16	520		
55	770	15	510		
54	770	14	510		
53	760	13	500		
52	760	12	490		
51	750	11	480		
50	740	10	480		
49	740	9	470		
48	730	8	460		
47	730	7	450		
46	720	6	450		
45	710	5	440		
44	710	4	430		
43	700	3	430		
42	700	2	420		
41	690	1	410		
40	680	0	400		
39	680	−1	400		
38	670	−2	390		
37	670	−3	380		
36	660	−4	380		

How Did You Do on the Subject Test in Physics?

After you score your test and analyze your performance, think about the following questions:

Did you run out of time before reaching the end of the test?

If so, you may need to pace yourself better. For example, maybe you spent too much time on one or two hard questions. A better approach might be to skip the ones you can't answer right away and try answering all the questions that remain on the test. Then if there's time, go back to the questions you skipped.

Did you take a long time reading the directions?

You will save time when you take the test by learning the directions to the Subject Test in Physics ahead of time. Each minute you spend reading directions during the test is a minute that you could use to answer questions.

How did you handle questions you were unsure of?

If you were able to eliminate one or more of the answer choices as wrong and guess from the remaining ones, your approach probably worked to your advantage. On the other hand, making haphazard guesses or omitting questions without trying to eliminate choices could cost you valuable points.

How difficult were the questions for you compared with other students who took the test?

Table A shows you how difficult the multiple-choice questions were for the group of students who took this test during its national administration. The right-hand column gives the percentage of students that answered each question correctly.

A question answered correctly by almost everyone in the group is obviously an easier question. For example, 78 percent of the students answered question 6 correctly. But only 25 percent answered question 43 correctly.

Keep in mind that these percentages are based on just one group of students. They would probably be different with another group of students taking the test.

If you missed several easier questions, go back and try to find out why: Did the questions cover material you haven't yet reviewed? Did you misunderstand the directions?

Answer Explanations

For Practice Test 2

Question 1

Choice (D) is the correct answer. During a phase change, the temperature of the substance remains constant, which is a plateau on the graph. Water boiling is a phase change from liquid to gas and thus must be the higher temperature plateau.

Question 2

Choice (C) is the correct answer. While the substance is getting warmer, the graph will have a positive slope. Since this is the liquid phase, it must be the middle section with a positive slope.

Question 3

Choice (B) is the correct answer. During a phase change, the temperature of the substance remains constant, which is a plateau on the graph. Ice melting is a phase change from solid to liquid and thus must be the plateau for the lower temperature.

Question 4

Choice (A) is the correct answer. The average kinetic energy of molecules is directly proportional to the temperature of a gas. Since the temperature remains constant, the average kinetic energy will remain constant.

Question 5

Choice (B) is the correct answer. Work is done on or by the gas ($W = \pm P\Delta V$) when the volume of the gas changes; therefore, no work will be done on or by the gas during a constant volume process.

Question 6

Choice (D) is the correct answer. The stone is in free fall, so its acceleration is constant throughout and therefore has the same value at both points Q and R.

Question 7

Choice (B) is the correct answer. Potential energy is directly proportional to height ($PE = mgh$). Since point Q is at twice the height of point R, the stone has twice the potential energy at point Q as it has at point R.

Question 8

Choice (A) is the correct answer. When a block is sliding down the incline, the net force will be $F = mg\sin\theta$, where θ is the angle of inclination with the horizontal. So the magnitude of the net force, its direction (along the incline), and the angle of the net force with respect to the path of motion (zero, since the net force is in the same direction as the motion) will all remain constant.

Question 9

Choice (C) is the correct answer. As the satellite moves at constant speed in the circular orbit, the magnitude of the net force remains constant according to the equation $F = \frac{mv^2}{r}$. The net force during uniform circular motion is always perpendicular to the velocity of the satellite, so the angle with respect to the path of motion remains constant. Since the net force always points toward the center of the circle as the satellite travels along the arc of the circle, the direction of the net force will be changing.

Question 10

Choice (B) is the correct answer. The projectile is in free fall, so the net force is the gravitational pull of Earth. Therefore, the magnitude and direction of the net force remain constant. However, since the direction of motion changes (from going up to going down), the angle of the net force with respect to the path of motion is changing.

Question 11

Choice (A) is the correct answer. As the pendulum swings upward toward its highest point, the height of the pendulum is increasing. Since the height of the pendulum is directly proportional to its gravitational potential energy, this energy increases as the pendulum swings upward.

Question 12

Choice (D) is the correct answer. The fission of uranium is a nuclear reaction, so it converts the nuclear potential energy that was holding the uranium nucleus together into electromagnetic radiation and kinetic energy of the subsequent fission products.

Question 13

Choice (A) is the correct answer. A glowing light bulb filament gives off white light that is made up of a continuous spectrum.

Question 14

Choice (B) is the correct answer. Gas discharge gives off a bright-line spectrum that can be used to identify the type of gas, such as the neon in the sign in this example.

Question 15

Choice (C) is the correct answer. Electric point charges create electric fields, so there will be a nonzero electric field near an electric point charge. Choice (D) has parallel plates with charges of equal magnitude and the <u>same</u> sign, so their electric fields midway between them cancel out.

Question 16

Choice (B) is the correct answer. There will always be a magnetic field surrounding a bar magnet. Choice (E) has parallel wires with currents of equal magnitude and in the <u>same</u> direction, so their magnetic fields midway between them cancel out.

Question 17

Choice (E) is the correct answer. Using the right-hand rule, a loop in the plane of the page with a counterclockwise current will create a magnetic field at the center of the loop that is directed out of the page.

Question 18

Choice (B) is the correct answer. Using the right-hand rule, the magnetic field created by wire 1 in the region of wire 2 is directed out of the page. Using the right-hand rule again, with the magnetic field out of the page and the current in wire 2 toward the top of the page, the force on wire 2 will be directed toward the right.

Question 19

Choice (A) is the correct answer. In order for the electric field to be zero at point P, the fields from the two charges must be equal in magnitude and in opposite directions. That will occur with two charges that are equal in magnitude and sign. For choice (A), the field from the charge on the left will point toward the right at point P, and the field from the charge on the right will point toward the left at point P, so the two fields cancel out. For choices (B) and (C), the fields from both charges will point toward the right and therefore cannot cancel out.

Question 20

Choice (C) is the correct answer. To create an electric field with the largest magnitude, the two fields should point in the same direction and be created by charges of the largest magnitude. Two opposite charges will point in the same direction at point P. The opposite charges with the largest magnitude are in choice (C).

Question 21

Choice (A) is the correct answer. Loudness corresponds to the energy of a sound wave. The energy of a wave is proportional to the square of the amplitude, so the loudness of a sound wave is determined by amplitude.

Question 22

Choice (B) is the correct answer. If the length of the string is fixed, the wavelength of the fundamental standing wave in the vibrating string will stay the same. As the tension in the string is increased, the wave speed will increase. If the wave speed increases and the wavelength remains the same, the frequency of vibration will increase, which increases the pitch of the sound heard.

Question 23

Choice (A) is the correct answer. The weight must point down, and the normal force must point up. Since force P is pushing the block to the right, P must point toward the right. Since the block is moving to the right, the frictional force f must point toward the left (opposite the direction of motion).

Question 24

Choice (D) is the correct answer. The graph shows an object in simple harmonic motion, so there must be a restoring force acting on the ball. For ball I there is a constant force, not one that returns the ball to equilibrium. Ball III attached to a vertical spring has a restoring spring force. Ball II in a ripple tank is possible as the ball oscillates between crests.

Question 25

Choice (A) is the correct answer. Power is the rate at which work is done. The work done in running up the steps will be equal to the increase in the gravitational potential energy of the person. And since the people all run to the same height in the same amount of time, the person with the greatest mass will also expend the greatest average power according to the equation $P = \dfrac{W}{t} = \dfrac{\Delta U}{t} = \dfrac{mg\Delta h}{t}$. So the person with the greatest mass (the heaviest student) will expend the greatest average power.

Question 26

Choice (E) is the correct answer. The gravitational force on the box is exerted vertically. This force can be separated into two components: $mg\sin\theta$ parallel to and down the incline and $mg\cos\theta$ perpendicular to and into the incline. Since the acceleration of the block is zero, the normal force is perpendicular to the incline and is equal in magnitude to the gravitational component perpendicular to the incline, $mg\cos\theta$.

Question 27

Choice (E) is the correct answer. The box is at rest on the incline, so the acceleration and the net force are zero. Since the net force is zero, it has no direction.

Question 28

Choice (E) is the correct answer. A ray that enters the lens parallel to the principal axis will be refracted through one of the two focus points, so choices (A) and (B) are possible. A ray that enters through a focal point will be refracted parallel to the principal axis, so choice (C) is possible. A ray that enters through the center of the lens will pass straight through, so choice (D) is possible.

Question 29

Choice (A) is the correct answer. Light is a transverse wave, and sound is a longitudinal wave. Polarization can only occur for transverse waves.

Question 30

Choice (C) is the correct answer. A wave that passes through a small opening will be diffracted, so I is correct. The waves from the two slits will create an interference pattern, so II is correct. The wavelength of the light does not change, so III is not correct.

Question 31

Choice (A) is the correct answer. As an object moves in a circle, the direction of motion and thus the linear momentum changes in direction. Energy is a scalar and does not have a direction, so choices (C) and (D) are incorrect. The altitude and thus the potential energy is constant in magnitude for an object that is moving in a circle, so choice (B) is incorrect. An object moving in a circle experiences a centripetal acceleration, so choice (E) is incorrect.

Question 32

Choice (C) is the correct answer. Both balls start with the same speed and thus the same initial kinetic energy. Both balls end up falling through the same height and thus have the same amount of potential energy transferred into kinetic energy. Therefore, both balls end up with the same final kinetic energy and the same final speed.

Question 33

Choice (E) is the correct answer. Any change in speed or direction of motion is evidence of an acceleration. So if the acceleration is zero, the object maintains constant speed and direction of motion.

Question 34

Choice (E) is the correct answer. The amount of static charge buildup is affected by the material involved, how much rubbing occurs, and air humidity, so choices (A), (B), and (D) affect the size of the shock. The part of the car touched might be a conductor or a nonconductor and might be shaped like a lightning rod, so choice (C) also affects the size of the shock.

Question 35

Choice (D) is the correct answer. Power dissipated in a circuit can be calculated according to the equation $P = I^2R$. So power dissipated is greater when the product of current squared and resistance is greater. Since the 12Ω resistor is the largest resistor and has the entire current I, it must dissipate the greatest power in this circuit.

Question 36

Choice (D) is the correct answer. To determine the resistance of an object, according to Ohm's law, you need to know the potential difference across the coil and the current through it. So you need a voltmeter and an ammeter.

Question 37

Choice (B) is the correct answer. The graph starts at the origin, which is the entrance to the tunnel; the tunnel is straight; and the mouse is inside the tunnel. Therefore, the displacement of the mouse shown in the graph represents the mouse's position inside the tunnel. So the greatest displacement of the mouse will also be its farthest position into the tunnel.

Question 38

Choice (B) is the correct answer. The average speed will be the total distance traveled divided by the total time of travel. From 10 s to 20 s, the displacement does not change, so the distance moved is zero. From 20 s to 35 s, the displacement changes from 2 m to 3 m, so the distance moved is 1 m. Therefore, the average speed is equal to (1 m)/(35 s – 10 s) = 1/25 m/s.

Question 39

Choice (A) is the correct answer. The average velocity will be the total displacement traveled divided by the total time of travel. Since the mouse ends up back at the entrance to the tunnel, the total displacement and thus the average velocity is zero.

Question 40

Choice (A) is the correct answer. As light from the bird enters the water, the light will be refracted toward the normal line, with a ray from the near end of the bird refracted less (or zero if right overhead) than a ray from the far end of the bird. Extrapolating these two underwater rays back out of the water, a bird of the same will seem to be farther away, making the bird appear higher than it is—so I is correct. This is not an image from a mirror or lens, so it is not inverted—so II is incorrect. Since the bird is directly above the diver's feet, the light will not be totally reflected.

Question 41

Choice (B) is the correct answer. Using the equation for wavelength of light as it enters water from air, $\lambda_m = \frac{\lambda}{n_m} = \frac{\lambda}{4/3} = \frac{3\lambda}{4}$. Alternately, using the equation relating velocity and index of refraction, $n_{air}/n_{water} = 1/(4/3) = 3/4 = v_{water}/v_{air} = (\lambda_{water}/f)/(\lambda_{air}/f) = \lambda_{water}/\lambda_{air}$ giving $\lambda_{water} = 3\lambda_{air}/4$.

Question 42

Choice (C) is the correct answer. The law of conservation of charge states that the charge of an isolated system does not change. So the total net charge of the objects is the same before and after interaction.

Question 43

Choice (C) is the correct answer. The existence of the electron cloud is a result of the wave properties of electrons.

Question 44

Choice (A) is the correct answer. When the temperature of a superconducting material drops below its critical temperature, its resistance becomes zero.

Question 45

Choice (C) is the correct answer. To make one rotation, it takes

24 hours = 24 hr × 60$\frac{min}{hr}$ × 60$\frac{s}{min}$ = 86,400 s. So the angular velocity would be 1 rev/86,400 s = 1.2 × 10⁻⁵ rev/s.

Question 46

Choice (C) is the correct answer. When adding two values, you also add the uncertainties. Thus, 0.3 + 0.2 = 0.5.

Question 47

Choice (E) is the correct answer. The units would be $\frac{kg \cdot m/s^2 \cdot m}{s} = \frac{N \cdot m}{s} = \frac{J}{s} = W$.

Question 48

Choice (A) is the correct answer. The modern view of the standard model of particles and fields postulates the existence of quarks.

Question 49

Choice (E) is the correct answer. Increasing the speed of coil 1 will increase the rate of change of magnetic flux and therefore the induced current at coil 2. Both increasing the number of coils in coil 1 and connecting it to a battery with a larger emf will increase the magnitude of the magnetic flux at coil 2. Therefore, all three of these changes will increase the induced current in coil 2.

Question 50

Choice (A) is the correct answer. The equation for the electric force is $F = \dfrac{kQ_1 Q_2}{r^2}$. So the graph of F as a function of r would decrease as the inverse square of the distance between the charges.

Question 51

Choice (C) is the correct answer. Electric forces still follow Newton's third law, so if X exerts a force of F on Y, then Y also exerts a force of F on X.

Question 52

Choice (C) is the correct answer. Using the equation for the energy of a photon, $E = hf$ and $c = \lambda f \therefore f = \dfrac{c}{\lambda} \therefore E = h\dfrac{c}{\lambda} \therefore \lambda = \dfrac{hc}{E}$.

Question 53

Choice (B) is the correct answer. Using Einstein's equation,
$E = m_0 c^2 = (9 \times 10^{-31} \text{ kg})(3 \times 10^8 \text{ m/s})^2 = 81 \times 10^{-15} \text{ Nm} = 8.1 \times 10^{-14} \text{ J} \approx 1.0 \times 10^{-13} \text{ J}$.

Question 54

Choice (A) is the correct answer. Newton's law of universal gravitation can be used to determine the acceleration due to gravity:
$F = G\dfrac{M_E m}{R_E^2} = mg \therefore g = \dfrac{GM_E}{R_E^2}$. So if the radius is doubled and all else stays the same,
$g' = \dfrac{GM_E}{(2R_E)^2} = \dfrac{GM_E}{4R_E^2} = \dfrac{g}{4}$.

Question 55

Choice (D) is the correct answer. Using the equation for centripetal acceleration,
$a = \dfrac{v^2}{r} \therefore a' = \dfrac{(3v)^2}{3r} = \dfrac{9v^2}{3r} = 3a$.

Question 56

Choice (D) is the correct answer. The kinetic energy when it strikes the ground will be
equal to the potential energy of the ball when it is dropped:
$PE = mgh = (10 \text{ kg})(10 \text{ m/s}^2)(100 \text{ m}) = 10,000 \text{ J}.$

Question 57

Choice (C) is the correct answer. The time of fall can be found in the vertical direction of motion. Since the initial vertical velocity is zero, you can use the equation

$$d = v_1 t + \frac{1}{2}at^2 = \frac{1}{2}at^2 \therefore t = \sqrt{\frac{2d}{a}} \therefore t = \sqrt{\frac{2(5m)}{(10m/s^2)}} = 1 \text{ s}.$$

The horizontal distance then can be calculated using $x = v_x t = \left(2\frac{m}{s}\right)$
$(1 \ s) = 2 \text{ m}$

Question 58

Choice (D) is the correct answer. At the highest point, the vertical component of a projectile's velocity is zero, so its velocity vector is horizontal. Since gravity is the only force acting on the projectile, the projectile's acceleration vector points down.

Question 59

Choice (C) is the correct answer. By definition, a completely inelastic collision occurs when two objects stick together.

Question 60

Choice (C) is the correct answer. Using conservation of momentum for an inelastic collision, $m_1 v_1 + m_2 v_2 = (m_1 + m_2)v_f$. Since the beanbag drops straight down and the car moves horizontally, the initial speed for the beanbag is set to zero:

$$m_1 v_1 = (m_1 + m_2) \therefore v_f = \frac{m_1 v_1}{(m_1 + m_2)} = \frac{(0.6\,\text{kg})\left(2\frac{m}{s}\right)}{(0.6\,\text{kg} + 0.2\,\text{kg})} = 1.5 \text{ m/s}.$$

Question 61

Choice (E) is the correct answer. The average acceleration can be calculated using change in speed divided by time. The average net force can be calculated by multiplying the average acceleration by the mass. The average power can be calculated either by dividing the change in kinetic energy by the time or by using the force and distance to calculate work and dividing by time to calculate the average power.

Question 62

Choice (A) is the correct answer. The wave speed is determined by the medium, so this stays the same. If the wave speed and frequency stay the same, the wavelength stays the same. If the frequency stays the same and the amplitude of the transverse wave increases, then the rod ends must move a greater distance in a direction perpendicular to the direction of travel of the wave in the same amount of time, so the average speed of the rod ends will increase.

Question 63

Choice (A) is the correct answer. Since the wave is moving toward the right, the points P and Q will next be at the position that is currently on their left. So P will move up and Q will move down.

Question 64

Choice (B) is the correct answer. The truck is creating waves at a constant rate. However, since the truck is moving, each wave is closer to the previous wave than if the truck were stationary. This will cause the observer to detect a decrease in wavelength and therefore an increase in frequency for the wave, since wave speed is unchanged.

Question 65

Choice (E) is the correct answer. All waves carry energy and momentum through a medium. A longitudinal wave such as a sound wave creates regions of compressions and rarefactions as it travels through a medium. Accordingly, sound waves exert pressure.

Question 66

Choice (A) is the correct answer. For a plane mirror, the image distance is equal to the object distance. So the point where the two arrows meet must be the farthest point from the mirror and the small arrow must still be below the longer arrow. That is only true for choice (A).

Question 67

Choice (E) is the correct answer. If the light rays are diverging, we know the light source is inside the focal point of the mirror. To create a parallel beam of light, the light source needs to be at the focal point. This can be done by either moving the light source away from the mirror to the focal point (II) or moving the focal point closer to the mirror by decreasing the radius of curvature for the mirror (III).

Question 68

Choice (E) is the correct answer. Since both cars are moving in the same direction, both velocities are positive. Using conservation of momentum for an inelastic collision,

$$m_1 v_1 + m_2 v_2 = (m_1 + m_2)v_f \therefore v_f = \frac{m_1 v_1 + m_2 v_2}{(m_1 + m_2)}$$

$$= \frac{(2 \text{ kg})(1 \text{ m/s}) + (3 \text{ kg})(3 \text{ m/s})}{(2 \text{ kg} + 3 \text{ kg})}$$

$$= 2.2 \text{ m/s.}$$

Question 69

Choice (B) is the correct answer. For this setup, the mass of the spring scale is not a factor. The reading of the spring scale is equal to the weight of the block. So the mass of the block is

$$W = mg \therefore m = \frac{W}{g} = \frac{(10\text{N})}{(10\text{m/s}^2)} = 1.0 \text{ kg.}$$

Question 70

Choice (A) is the correct answer. The direction of the electric field at any point along the electric field lines is tangent to the electric field line through that point. The electric force on a positive charge is in the same direction as the electric field and thus along the same tangent. The force on a positive charge will be away from the $+Q$ charge and toward the $-Q$ charge.

Question 71

Choice (D) is the correct answer. There will be an induced current in the circuit with the ammeter only if the magnetic flux through the coil is changing. This will only occur when the current in the top coil is changing, and it will occur for either direction of changing current in the first coil.

Question 72

Choice (E) is the correct answer. The amount of heat absorbed by block A is equal to the amount of heat lost by block B. The heat flow for block A is given by $Q_A = Mc\Delta T_A$ and the heat flow for block B is given by $Q_B = \frac{M}{2} \frac{c}{2}\Delta T_B$. By conservation of energy, $Q_A = Mc\Delta T_A$. So

$$-Q_B - \frac{M}{2} \frac{c}{2}\Delta T_B \text{ or } \Delta T_B = -4\Delta T_A \therefore \Delta T_B = -4(20 \text{ K}) \therefore \Delta T_B = -80 \text{ K.}$$

Question 73

Choice (D) is the correct answer. To determine the acceleration of the satellites, $F = G\dfrac{Mm}{R^2} = ma \therefore a = \dfrac{GM}{R^2}$. Since both orbits have the same radius, both satellites experience the same acceleration. Since the accelerations are both the same, applying Newton's second law, the satellite with twice the mass will experience twice the force.

Question 74

Choice (A) is the correct answer. Since the ball is thrown at an angle, the velocity continually has a horizontal component and thus the ball still has kinetic energy at the highest point of the trajectory when the vertical component of velocity is zero.

Question 75

Choice (C) is the correct answer. Both the force of the seat and the force of Earth's gravity are exerted on the astronaut. So the net force in the upward direction on the astronaut is $F_{net} = F_{seat} - F_g = 4Mg - Mg = 3Mg$.

The acceleration of the astronaut would be

$$F_{net} = ma \therefore a = \frac{F_{net}}{m} = \frac{3Mg}{M} = 3g.$$

CollegeBoard

SAT Subject Tests™

COMPLETE MARK ● **EXAMPLES OF INCOMPLETE MARKS**

You must use a No. 2 pencil and marks must be complete. Do not use a mechanical pencil. It is very important that you fill in the entire circle darkly and completely. If you change your response, erase as completely as possible. Incomplete marks or erasures may affect your score.

1 Your Name:
(Print)

Last   First   M.I.

I agree to the conditions on the front and back of the SAT Subject Tests™ book. I also agree with the SAT Test Security and Fairness policies and understand that any violation of these policies will result in score cancellation and may result in reporting of certain violations to law enforcement.

Signature:

Today's Date: ___/___/___
MM   DD   YY

Home Address:
(Print)
Number and Street   City   State/Country   Zip Code

Phone: (   )

Test Center:
(Print)   City   State/Country

2 YOUR NAME

Last Name (First 6 Letters)   First Name (First 4 Letters)   Mid. Init.

3 DATE OF BIRTH

MONTH	DAY	YEAR
Jan		
Feb		
Mar		
Apr		
May		
Jun		
Jul		
Aug		
Sep		
Oct		
Nov		
Dec		

4 REGISTRATION NUMBER
(Copy from Admission Ticket.)

5 ZIP CODE

6 TEST CENTER
(Supplied by Test Center Supervisor.)

Important: Fill in items 8 and 9 exactly as shown on the back of test book.

8 BOOK CODE
(Copy and grid as on back of test book.)

7 TEST BOOK SERIAL NUMBER
(Copy from front of test book.)

9 BOOK ID
(Copy from back of test book.)

PLEASE MAKE SURE to fill in these fields completely and correctly. If they are not correct, we won't be able to score your test(s)!

FOR OFFICIAL USE ONLY

103648-77191 • NS1114C1085 • Printed in U.S.A.

194415-001   1 2 3 4 5 A B C D E   Printed in the USA   ISD11312

783175

PLEASE DO NOT WRITE IN THIS AREA

SERIAL #

23459 College Board 15b-10820-Text

COMPLETE MARK ●   **EXAMPLES OF INCOMPLETE MARKS**

You must use a No. 2 pencil and marks must be complete. Do not use a mechanical pencil. *It is very important that you fill in the entire circle darkly and completely. If you change your response, erase as completely as possible. Incomplete marks or erasures may affect your score.*

- ○ Literature
- ○ Biology E
- ○ Biology M
- ○ Chemistry
- ○ Physics
- ○ Mathematics Level 1
- ○ Mathematics Level 2
- ○ U.S. History
- ○ World History
- ○ French
- ○ German
- ○ Italian
- ○ Latin
- ○ Modern Hebrew
- ○ Spanish
- ○ Chinese Listening
- ○ French Listening
- ○ German Listening
- ○ Japanese Listening
- ○ Korean Listening
- ○ Spanish Listening

Background Questions: ① ② ③ ④ ⑤ ⑥ ⑦ ⑧ ⑨

1–100 answer grid: A B C D E for questions 1 through 100.

PLEASE MAKE SURE to fill in these fields completely and correctly. If they are not correct, we won't be able to score your test(s)!

7 TEST BOOK SERIAL NUMBER (Copy from front of test book.)

8 BOOK CODE (Copy and grid as on back of test book.)

9 BOOK ID (Copy from back of test book.)

Quality Assurance Mark

Chemistry *Fill in circle CE only if II is correct explanation of I.

	I	II	CE*		I	II	CE*
101	T F	T F	○	109	T F	T F	○
102	T F	T F	○	110	T F	T F	○
103	T F	T F	○	111	T F	T F	○
104	T F	T F	○	112	T F	T F	○
105	T F	T F	○	113	T F	T F	○
106	T F	T F	○	114	T F	T F	○
107	T F	T F	○	115	T F	T F	○
108	T F	T F	○				

FOR OFFICIAL USE ONLY

R/C	W/S1	FS/S2	CS/S3	WS

CERTIFICATION STATEMENT Copy the statement below and sign your name as you would an official document.

I hereby agree to the conditions set forth online at sat.collegeboard.org and in any paper registration materials given to me and certify that I am the person whose name, address and signature appear on this answer sheet.

Signature _____   Date _____

Page 2

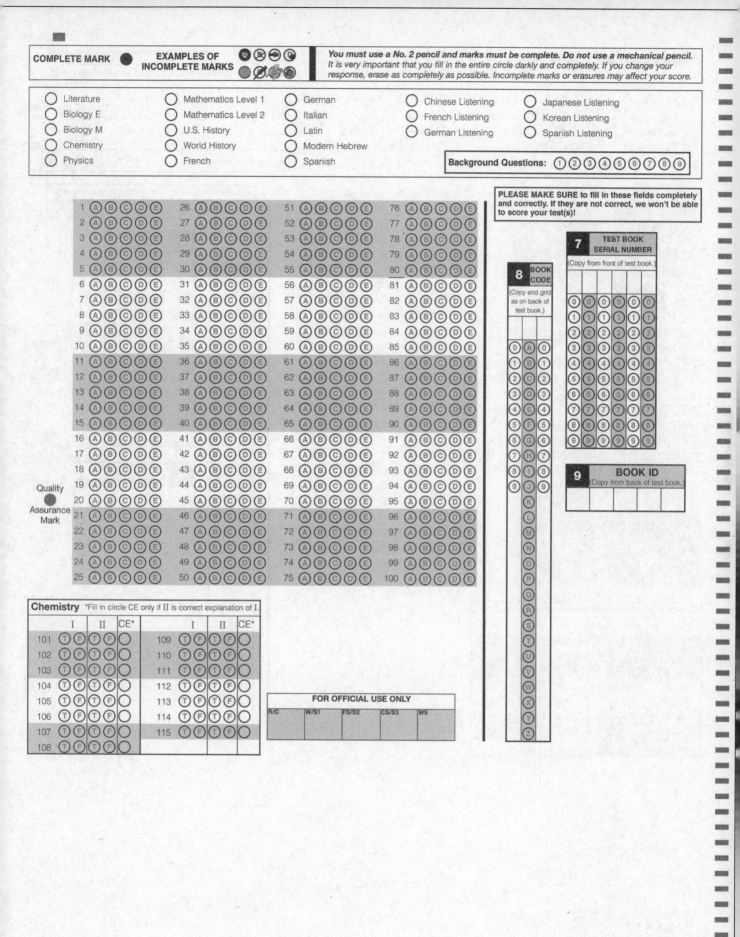

23459 College Board 15b-10820-Text

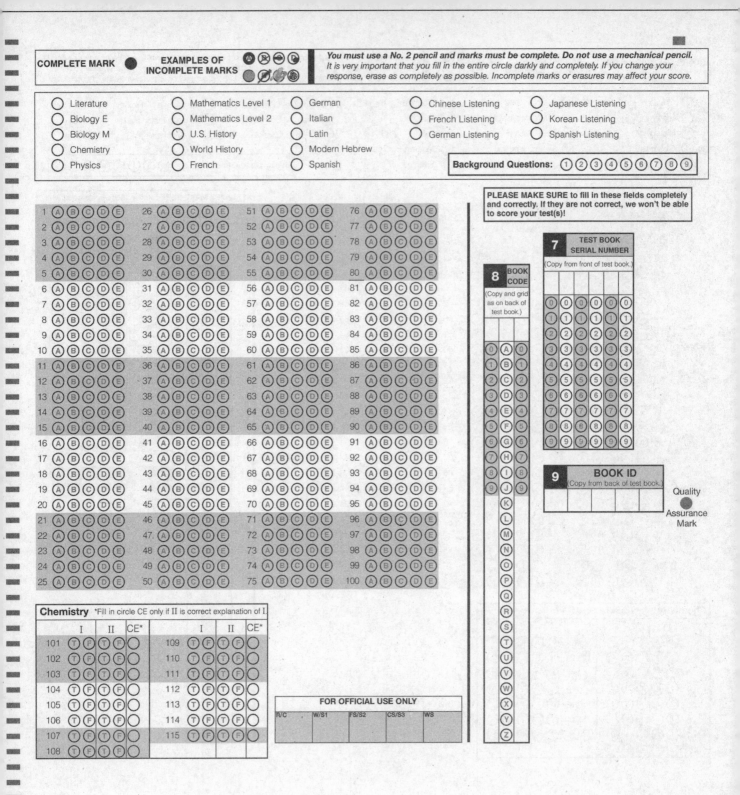

○ Literature
○ Biology E
○ Biology M
○ Chemistry
○ Physics

○ Mathematics Level 1
○ Mathematics Level 2
○ U.S. History
○ World History
○ French

○ German
○ Italian
○ Latin
○ Modern Hebrew
○ Spanish

○ Chinese Listening
○ French Listening
○ German Listening

○ Japanese Listening
○ Korean Listening
○ Spanish Listening

Background Questions: ① ② ③ ④ ⑤ ⑥ ⑦ ⑧ ⑨

PLEASE MAKE SURE to fill in these fields completely and correctly. If they are not correct, we won't be able to score your test(s)!

7 TEST BOOK SERIAL NUMBER (Copy from front of test book.)

8 BOOK CODE (Copy and grid as on back of test book.)

9 BOOK ID (Copy from back of test book.)

Quality Assurance Mark

Chemistry *Fill in circle CE only if II is correct explanation of I.

	I	II	CE*		I	II	CE*
101	T F	T F	○	109	T F	T F	○
102	T F	T F	○	110	T F	T F	○
103	T F	T F	○	111	T F	T F	○
104	T F	T F	○	112	T F	T F	○
105	T F	T F	○	113	T F	T F	○
106	T F	T F	○	114	T F	T F	○
107	T F	T F	○	115	T F	T F	○
108	T F	T F	○				

FOR OFFICIAL USE ONLY				
R/C	W/S1	FS/S2	CS/S3	WS

Page 4

PLEASE DO NOT WRITE IN THIS AREA

SERIAL #

23459 College Board 15b-10820-Text

CollegeBoard

SAT Subject Tests™

COMPLETE MARK ● EXAMPLES OF INCOMPLETE MARKS Ⓐ ⊗ ⊖ Ⓒ ⊘ ⊜

You must use a No. 2 pencil and marks must be complete. Do not use a mechanical pencil. It is very important that you fill in the entire circle darkly and completely. If you change your response, erase as completely as possible. Incomplete marks or erasures may affect your score.

1 Your Name:
(Print)

Last _____ First _____ M.I. _____

I agree to the conditions on the front and back of the SAT Subject Tests™ book. I also agree with the SAT Test Security and Fairness policies and understand that any violation of these policies will result in score cancellation and may result in reporting of certain violations to law enforcement.

Signature: _____ Today's Date: ___/___/___ MM DD YY

Home Address: _____
(Print) Number and Street | City | State/Country | Zip Code

Phone: ( ) _____ Test Center: _____
(Print) | City | State/Country

2 YOUR NAME
Last Name (First 6 Letters) | First Name (First 4 Letters) | Mid. Init.

3 DATE OF BIRTH
MONTH | DAY | YEAR

Jan, Feb, Mar, Apr, May, Jun, Jul, Aug, Sep, Oct, Nov, Dec

4 REGISTRATION NUMBER
(Copy from Admission Ticket.)

5 ZIP CODE

6 TEST CENTER
(Supplied by Test Center Supervisor.)

Important: Fill in items 8 and 9 exactly as shown on the back of test book.

7 TEST BOOK SERIAL NUMBER
(Copy from front of test book.)

8 BOOK CODE
(Copy and grid as on back of test book.)

9 BOOK ID
(Copy from back of test book.)

PLEASE MAKE SURE to fill in these fields completely and correctly. If they are not correct, we won't be able to score your test(s)!

FOR OFFICIAL USE ONLY
0 1 2 3 4 5 6
0 1 2 3 4 5 6
0 1 2 3 4 5 6

103648-77191 • NS1114C1085 • Printed in U.S.A.

© 2015 The College Board. College Board, SAT, and the acorn logo are registered trademarks of the College Board. SAT Subject Tests is a trademark owned by the College Board.

194415-001 1 2 3 4 5 A B C D E Printed in the USA ISD11312

783175

PLEASE DO NOT WRITE IN THIS AREA

SERIAL #

23459 College Board 15b-10820-Text

COMPLETE MARK ●	EXAMPLES OF INCOMPLETE MARKS ⓐ ⊗ ⊖ ⓒ ⊘ ⊜	You must use a No. 2 pencil and marks must be complete. Do not use a mechanical pencil. It is very important that you fill in the entire circle darkly and completely. If you change your response, erase as completely as possible. Incomplete marks or erasures may affect your score.

○ Literature
○ Biology E
○ Biology M
○ Chemistry
○ Physics

○ Mathematics Level 1
○ Mathematics Level 2
○ U.S. History
○ World History
○ French

○ German
○ Italian
○ Latin
○ Modern Hebrew
○ Spanish

○ Chinese Listening
○ French Listening
○ German Listening

○ Japanese Listening
○ Korean Listening
○ Spanish Listening

Background Questions: ① ② ③ ④ ⑤ ⑥ ⑦ ⑧ ⑨

1 (A)(B)(C)(D)(E)   26 (A)(B)(C)(D)(E)   51 (A)(B)(C)(D)(E)   76 (A)(B)(C)(D)(E)
2 (A)(B)(C)(D)(E)   27 (A)(B)(C)(D)(E)   52 (A)(B)(C)(D)(E)   77 (A)(B)(C)(D)(E)
3 (A)(B)(C)(D)(E)   28 (A)(B)(C)(D)(E)   53 (A)(B)(C)(D)(E)   78 (A)(B)(C)(D)(E)
4 (A)(B)(C)(D)(E)   29 (A)(B)(C)(D)(E)   54 (A)(B)(C)(D)(E)   79 (A)(B)(C)(D)(E)
5 (A)(B)(C)(D)(E)   30 (A)(B)(C)(D)(E)   55 (A)(B)(C)(D)(E)   80 (A)(B)(C)(D)(E)
6 (A)(B)(C)(D)(E)   31 (A)(B)(C)(D)(E)   56 (A)(B)(C)(D)(E)   81 (A)(B)(C)(D)(E)
7 (A)(B)(C)(D)(E)   32 (A)(B)(C)(D)(E)   57 (A)(B)(C)(D)(E)   82 (A)(B)(C)(D)(E)
8 (A)(B)(C)(D)(E)   33 (A)(B)(C)(D)(E)   58 (A)(B)(C)(D)(E)   83 (A)(B)(C)(D)(E)
9 (A)(B)(C)(D)(E)   34 (A)(B)(C)(D)(E)   59 (A)(B)(C)(D)(E)   84 (A)(B)(C)(D)(E)
10 (A)(B)(C)(D)(E)   35 (A)(B)(C)(D)(E)   60 (A)(B)(C)(D)(E)   85 (A)(B)(C)(D)(E)
11 (A)(B)(C)(D)(E)   36 (A)(B)(C)(D)(E)   61 (A)(B)(C)(D)(E)   86 (A)(B)(C)(D)(E)
12 (A)(B)(C)(D)(E)   37 (A)(B)(C)(D)(E)   62 (A)(B)(C)(D)(E)   87 (A)(B)(C)(D)(E)
13 (A)(B)(C)(D)(E)   38 (A)(B)(C)(D)(E)   63 (A)(B)(C)(D)(E)   88 (A)(B)(C)(D)(E)
14 (A)(B)(C)(D)(E)   39 (A)(B)(C)(D)(E)   64 (A)(B)(C)(D)(E)   89 (A)(B)(C)(D)(E)
15 (A)(B)(C)(D)(E)   40 (A)(B)(C)(D)(E)   65 (A)(B)(C)(D)(E)   90 (A)(B)(C)(D)(E)
16 (A)(B)(C)(D)(E)   41 (A)(B)(C)(D)(E)   66 (A)(B)(C)(D)(E)   91 (A)(B)(C)(D)(E)
17 (A)(B)(C)(D)(E)   42 (A)(B)(C)(D)(E)   67 (A)(B)(C)(D)(E)   92 (A)(B)(C)(D)(E)
18 (A)(B)(C)(D)(E)   43 (A)(B)(C)(D)(E)   68 (A)(B)(C)(D)(E)   93 (A)(B)(C)(D)(E)
19 (A)(B)(C)(D)(E)   44 (A)(B)(C)(D)(E)   69 (A)(B)(C)(D)(E)   94 (A)(B)(C)(D)(E)
20 (A)(B)(C)(D)(E)   45 (A)(B)(C)(D)(E)   70 (A)(B)(C)(D)(E)   95 (A)(B)(C)(D)(E)
21 (A)(B)(C)(D)(E)   46 (A)(B)(C)(D)(E)   71 (A)(B)(C)(D)(E)   96 (A)(B)(C)(D)(E)
22 (A)(B)(C)(D)(E)   47 (A)(B)(C)(D)(E)   72 (A)(B)(C)(D)(E)   97 (A)(B)(C)(D)(E)
23 (A)(B)(C)(D)(E)   48 (A)(B)(C)(D)(E)   73 (A)(B)(C)(D)(E)   98 (A)(B)(C)(D)(E)
24 (A)(B)(C)(D)(E)   49 (A)(B)(C)(D)(E)   74 (A)(B)(C)(D)(E)   99 (A)(B)(C)(D)(E)
25 (A)(B)(C)(D)(E)   50 (A)(B)(C)(D)(E)   75 (A)(B)(C)(D)(E)   100 (A)(B)(C)(D)(E)

PLEASE MAKE SURE to fill in these fields completely and correctly. If they are not correct, we won't be able to score your test(s)!

7 TEST BOOK SERIAL NUMBER (Copy from front of test book.)

0 0 0 0 0 0
1 1 1 1 1 1
2 2 2 2 2 2
3 3 3 3 3 3
4 4 4 4 4 4
5 5 5 5 5 5
6 6 6 6 6 6
7 7 7 7 7 7
8 8 8 8 8 8
9 9 9 9 9 9

8 BOOK CODE (Copy and grid as on back of test book.)

0 A 0
1 B 1
2 C 2
3 D 3
4 E 4
5 F 5
6 G 6
7 H 7
8 I 8
9 J 9
K
L
M
N
O
P
Q
R
S
T
U
V
W
X
Y
Z

9 BOOK ID (Copy from back of test book.)

○ Quality Assurance Mark

Chemistry *Fill in circle CE only if II is correct explanation of I.

	I	II	CE*		I	II	CE*
101	(T)(F)	(T)(F)	○	109	(T)(F)	(T)(F)	○
102	(T)(F)	(T)(F)	○	110	(T)(F)	(T)(F)	○
103	(T)(F)	(T)(F)	○	111	(T)(F)	(T)(F)	○
104	(T)(F)	(T)(F)	○	112	(T)(F)	(T)(F)	○
105	(T)(F)	(T)(F)	○	113	(T)(F)	(T)(F)	○
106	(T)(F)	(T)(F)	○	114	(T)(F)	(T)(F)	○
107	(T)(F)	(T)(F)	○	115	(T)(F)	(T)(F)	○
108	(T)(F)	(T)(F)	○				

FOR OFFICIAL USE ONLY				
R/C	W/S1	FS/S2	CS/S3	WS

CERTIFICATION STATEMENT Copy the statement below and sign your name as you would an official document.

I hereby agree to the conditions set forth online at sat.collegeboard.org and in any paper registration materials given to me and certify that I am the person whose name, address and signature appear on this answer sheet.

_____

_____

_____

Signature _____   Date _____

Page 2

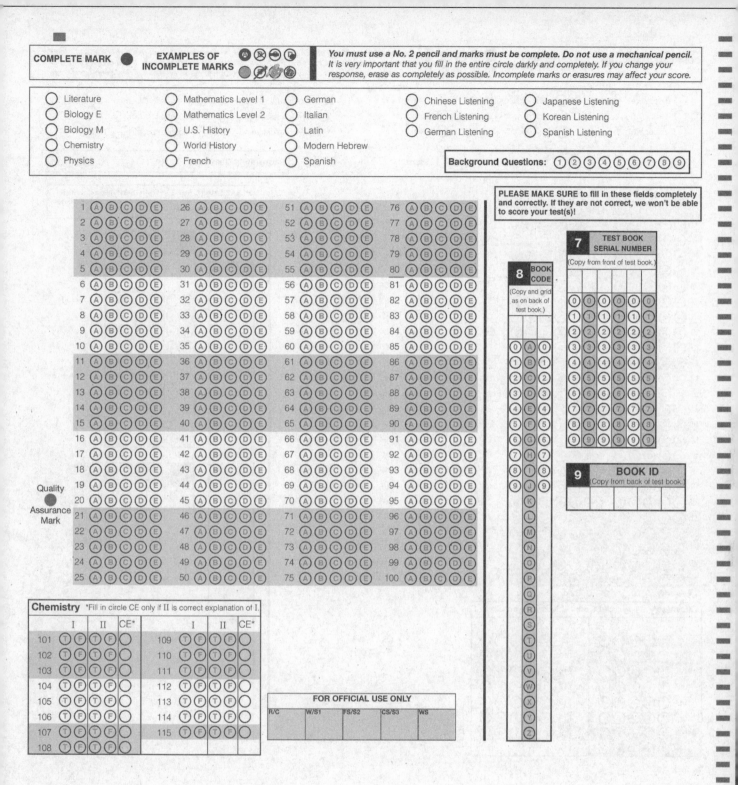

COMPLETE MARK ● EXAMPLES OF INCOMPLETE MARKS

You must use a No. 2 pencil and marks must be complete. Do not use a mechanical pencil. It is very important that you fill in the entire circle darkly and completely. If you change your response, erase as completely as possible. Incomplete marks or erasures may affect your score.

○ Literature
○ Biology E
○ Biology M
○ Chemistry
○ Physics
○ Mathematics Level 1
○ Mathematics Level 2
○ U.S. History
○ World History
○ French
○ German
○ Italian
○ Latin
○ Modern Hebrew
○ Spanish
○ Chinese Listening
○ French Listening
○ German Listening
○ Japanese Listening
○ Korean Listening
○ Spanish Listening

Background Questions: ① ② ③ ④ ⑤ ⑥ ⑦ ⑧ ⑨

PLEASE MAKE SURE to fill in these fields completely and correctly. If they are not correct, we won't be able to score your test(s)!

7 TEST BOOK SERIAL NUMBER
(Copy from front of test book.)

8 BOOK CODE
(Copy and grid as on back of test book.)

9 BOOK ID
(Copy from back of test book.)

Quality Assurance Mark

Chemistry *Fill in circle CE only if II is correct explanation of I.

	I	II	CE*		I	II	CE*
101	T F	T F	○	109	T F	T F	○
102	T F	T F	○	110	T F	T F	○
103	T F	T F	○	111	T F	T F	○
104	T F	T F	○	112	T F	T F	○
105	T F	T F	○	113	T F	T F	○
106	T F	T F	○	114	T F	T F	○
107	T F	T F	○	115	T F	T F	○
108	T F	T F	○				

FOR OFFICIAL USE ONLY				
R/C	W/S1	FS/S2	CS/S3	WS

Page 3

23459 College Board 15b-10820-Text

○ Literature
○ Biology E
○ Biology M
○ Chemistry
○ Physics

○ Mathematics Level 1
○ Mathematics Level 2
○ U.S. History
○ World History
○ French

○ German
○ Italian
○ Latin
○ Modern Hebrew
○ Spanish

○ Chinese Listening
○ French Listening
○ German Listening

○ Japanese Listening
○ Korean Listening
○ Spanish Listening

Background Questions: ① ② ③ ④ ⑤ ⑥ ⑦ ⑧ ⑨

PLEASE MAKE SURE to fill in these fields completely and correctly. If they are not correct, we won't be able to score your test(s)!

(Answer grid, questions 1–100, each with options A B C D E)

7 TEST BOOK SERIAL NUMBER (Copy from front of test book.)

8 BOOK CODE (Copy and grid as on back of test book.)

9 BOOK ID (Copy from back of test book.)

Quality Assurance Mark

Chemistry *Fill in circle CE only if II is correct explanation of I.

	I	II	CE*		I	II	CE*
101	T F	T F	○	109	T F	T F	○
102	T F	T F	○	110	T F	T F	○
103	T F	T F	○	111	T F	T F	○
104	T F	T F	○	112	T F	T F	○
105	T F	T F	○	113	T F	T F	○
106	T F	T F	○	114	T F	T F	○
107	T F	T F	○	115	T F	T F	○
108	T F	T F	○				

FOR OFFICIAL USE ONLY

R/C	W/S1	FS/S2	CS/S3	WS

Page 4

PLEASE DO NOT WRITE IN THIS AREA

SERIAL #

SAT Subject Tests™

1 Your Name:
(Print)

Last   First   M.I.

I agree to the conditions on the front and back of the SAT Subject Tests™ book. I also agree with the SAT Test Security and Fairness policies and understand that any violation of these policies will result in score cancellation and may result in reporting of certain violations to law enforcement.

Signature: _____   **Today's Date:** ___/___/___
                                                                                                          MM   DD   YY

Home Address: _____
(Print)   Number and Street   City   State/Country   Zip Code

Phone: (   ) _____   **Test Center:** _____
                                        (Print)   City   State/Country

2 YOUR NAME

Last Name (First 6 Letters) / First Name (First 4 Letters) / Mid. Init.

3 DATE OF BIRTH

MONTH | DAY | YEAR

Jan Feb Mar Apr May Jun Jul Aug Sep Oct Nov Dec

4 REGISTRATION NUMBER

(Copy from Admission Ticket.)

Important: Fill in items 8 and 9 exactly as shown on the back of test book.

7 TEST BOOK SERIAL NUMBER

(Copy from front of test book.)

8 BOOK CODE

(Copy and grid as on back of test book.)

0 A 0
1 B 1
2 C 2
3 D 3
4 E 4
5 F 5
6 G 6
7 H 7
8 I 8
9 J 9
K
L
M
N
O
P
Q
R
S
T
U
V
W
X
Y
Z

9 BOOK ID

(Copy from back of test book.)

PLEASE MAKE SURE to fill in these fields completely and correctly. If they are not correct, we won't be able to score your test(s)!

5 ZIP CODE

6 TEST CENTER

(Supplied by Test Center Supervisor.)

FOR OFFICIAL USE ONLY

0 1 2 3 4 5 6
0 1 2 3 4 5 6
0 1 2 3 4 5 6

103648-77191 • NS1114C1085 • Printed in U.S.A.

194415-001   1 2 3 4 5 A B C D E   Printed in the USA   ISD11312   783175

PLEASE DO NOT WRITE IN THIS AREA   **SERIAL #**

23459 College Board 15b-10820-Text

COMPLETE MARK ● EXAMPLES OF INCOMPLETE MARKS Ⓐ ⊗ ⊖ Ⓕ / Ⓒ

You must use a No. 2 pencil and marks must be complete. Do not use a mechanical pencil.
It is very important that you fill in the entire circle darkly and completely. If you change your response, erase as completely as possible. Incomplete marks or erasures may affect your score.

○ Literature
○ Biology E
○ Biology M
○ Chemistry
○ Physics

○ Mathematics Level 1
○ Mathematics Level 2
○ U.S. History
○ World History
○ French

○ German
○ Italian
○ Latin
○ Modern Hebrew
○ Spanish

○ Chinese Listening
○ French Listening
○ German Listening

○ Japanese Listening
○ Korean Listening
○ Spanish Listening

Background Questions: ① ② ③ ④ ⑤ ⑥ ⑦ ⑧ ⑨

PLEASE MAKE SURE to fill in these fields completely and correctly. If they are not correct, we won't be able to score your test(s)!

1 Ⓐ Ⓑ Ⓒ Ⓓ Ⓔ   26 Ⓐ Ⓑ Ⓒ Ⓓ Ⓔ   51 Ⓐ Ⓑ Ⓒ Ⓓ Ⓔ   76 Ⓐ Ⓑ Ⓒ Ⓓ Ⓔ
2 Ⓐ Ⓑ Ⓒ Ⓓ Ⓔ   27 Ⓐ Ⓑ Ⓒ Ⓓ Ⓔ   52 Ⓐ Ⓑ Ⓒ Ⓓ Ⓔ   77 Ⓐ Ⓑ Ⓒ Ⓓ Ⓔ
3 Ⓐ Ⓑ Ⓒ Ⓓ Ⓔ   28 Ⓐ Ⓑ Ⓒ Ⓓ Ⓔ   53 Ⓐ Ⓑ Ⓒ Ⓓ Ⓔ   78 Ⓐ Ⓑ Ⓒ Ⓓ Ⓔ
4 Ⓐ Ⓑ Ⓒ Ⓓ Ⓔ   29 Ⓐ Ⓑ Ⓒ Ⓓ Ⓔ   54 Ⓐ Ⓑ Ⓒ Ⓓ Ⓔ   79 Ⓐ Ⓑ Ⓒ Ⓓ Ⓔ
5 Ⓐ Ⓑ Ⓒ Ⓓ Ⓔ   30 Ⓐ Ⓑ Ⓒ Ⓓ Ⓔ   55 Ⓐ Ⓑ Ⓒ Ⓓ Ⓔ   80 Ⓐ Ⓑ Ⓒ Ⓓ Ⓔ
6 Ⓐ Ⓑ Ⓒ Ⓓ Ⓔ   31 Ⓐ Ⓑ Ⓒ Ⓓ Ⓔ   56 Ⓐ Ⓑ Ⓒ Ⓓ Ⓔ   81 Ⓐ Ⓑ Ⓒ Ⓓ Ⓔ
7 Ⓐ Ⓑ Ⓒ Ⓓ Ⓔ   32 Ⓐ Ⓑ Ⓒ Ⓓ Ⓔ   57 Ⓐ Ⓑ Ⓒ Ⓓ Ⓔ   82 Ⓐ Ⓑ Ⓒ Ⓓ Ⓔ
8 Ⓐ Ⓑ Ⓒ Ⓓ Ⓔ   33 Ⓐ Ⓑ Ⓒ Ⓓ Ⓔ   58 Ⓐ Ⓑ Ⓒ Ⓓ Ⓔ   83 Ⓐ Ⓑ Ⓒ Ⓓ Ⓔ
9 Ⓐ Ⓑ Ⓒ Ⓓ Ⓔ   34 Ⓐ Ⓑ Ⓒ Ⓓ Ⓔ   59 Ⓐ Ⓑ Ⓒ Ⓓ Ⓔ   84 Ⓐ Ⓑ Ⓒ Ⓓ Ⓔ
10 Ⓐ Ⓑ Ⓒ Ⓓ Ⓔ   35 Ⓐ Ⓑ Ⓒ Ⓓ Ⓔ   60 Ⓐ Ⓑ Ⓒ Ⓓ Ⓔ   85 Ⓐ Ⓑ Ⓒ Ⓓ Ⓔ
11 Ⓐ Ⓑ Ⓒ Ⓓ Ⓔ   36 Ⓐ Ⓑ Ⓒ Ⓓ Ⓔ   61 Ⓐ Ⓑ Ⓒ Ⓓ Ⓔ   86 Ⓐ Ⓑ Ⓒ Ⓓ Ⓔ
12 Ⓐ Ⓑ Ⓒ Ⓓ Ⓔ   37 Ⓐ Ⓑ Ⓒ Ⓓ Ⓔ   62 Ⓐ Ⓑ Ⓒ Ⓓ Ⓔ   87 Ⓐ Ⓑ Ⓒ Ⓓ Ⓔ
13 Ⓐ Ⓑ Ⓒ Ⓓ Ⓔ   38 Ⓐ Ⓑ Ⓒ Ⓓ Ⓔ   63 Ⓐ Ⓑ Ⓒ Ⓓ Ⓔ   88 Ⓐ Ⓑ Ⓒ Ⓓ Ⓔ
14 Ⓐ Ⓑ Ⓒ Ⓓ Ⓔ   39 Ⓐ Ⓑ Ⓒ Ⓓ Ⓔ   64 Ⓐ Ⓑ Ⓒ Ⓓ Ⓔ   89 Ⓐ Ⓑ Ⓒ Ⓓ Ⓔ
15 Ⓐ Ⓑ Ⓒ Ⓓ Ⓔ   40 Ⓐ Ⓑ Ⓒ Ⓓ Ⓔ   65 Ⓐ Ⓑ Ⓒ Ⓓ Ⓔ   90 Ⓐ Ⓑ Ⓒ Ⓓ Ⓔ
16 Ⓐ Ⓑ Ⓒ Ⓓ Ⓔ   41 Ⓐ Ⓑ Ⓒ Ⓓ Ⓔ   66 Ⓐ Ⓑ Ⓒ Ⓓ Ⓔ   91 Ⓐ Ⓑ Ⓒ Ⓓ Ⓔ
17 Ⓐ Ⓑ Ⓒ Ⓓ Ⓔ   42 Ⓐ Ⓑ Ⓒ Ⓓ Ⓔ   67 Ⓐ Ⓑ Ⓒ Ⓓ Ⓔ   92 Ⓐ Ⓑ Ⓒ Ⓓ Ⓔ
18 Ⓐ Ⓑ Ⓒ Ⓓ Ⓔ   43 Ⓐ Ⓑ Ⓒ Ⓓ Ⓔ   68 Ⓐ Ⓑ Ⓒ Ⓓ Ⓔ   93 Ⓐ Ⓑ Ⓒ Ⓓ Ⓔ
19 Ⓐ Ⓑ Ⓒ Ⓓ Ⓔ   44 Ⓐ Ⓑ Ⓒ Ⓓ Ⓔ   69 Ⓐ Ⓑ Ⓒ Ⓓ Ⓔ   94 Ⓐ Ⓑ Ⓒ Ⓓ Ⓔ
20 Ⓐ Ⓑ Ⓒ Ⓓ Ⓔ   45 Ⓐ Ⓑ Ⓒ Ⓓ Ⓔ   70 Ⓐ Ⓑ Ⓒ Ⓓ Ⓔ   95 Ⓐ Ⓑ Ⓒ Ⓓ Ⓔ
21 Ⓐ Ⓑ Ⓒ Ⓓ Ⓔ   46 Ⓐ Ⓑ Ⓒ Ⓓ Ⓔ   71 Ⓐ Ⓑ Ⓒ Ⓓ Ⓔ   96 Ⓐ Ⓑ Ⓒ Ⓓ Ⓔ
22 Ⓐ Ⓑ Ⓒ Ⓓ Ⓔ   47 Ⓐ Ⓑ Ⓒ Ⓓ Ⓔ   72 Ⓐ Ⓑ Ⓒ Ⓓ Ⓔ   97 Ⓐ Ⓑ Ⓒ Ⓓ Ⓔ
23 Ⓐ Ⓑ Ⓒ Ⓓ Ⓔ   48 Ⓐ Ⓑ Ⓒ Ⓓ Ⓔ   73 Ⓐ Ⓑ Ⓒ Ⓓ Ⓔ   98 Ⓐ Ⓑ Ⓒ Ⓓ Ⓔ
24 Ⓐ Ⓑ Ⓒ Ⓓ Ⓔ   49 Ⓐ Ⓑ Ⓒ Ⓓ Ⓔ   74 Ⓐ Ⓑ Ⓒ Ⓓ Ⓔ   99 Ⓐ Ⓑ Ⓒ Ⓓ Ⓔ
25 Ⓐ Ⓑ Ⓒ Ⓓ Ⓔ   50 Ⓐ Ⓑ Ⓒ Ⓓ Ⓔ   75 Ⓐ Ⓑ Ⓒ Ⓓ Ⓔ   100 Ⓐ Ⓑ Ⓒ Ⓓ Ⓔ

8 BOOK CODE (Copy and grid as on back of test book.)

0 Ⓐ 0
1 Ⓑ 1
2 Ⓒ 2
3 Ⓓ 3
4 Ⓔ 4
5 Ⓕ 5
6 Ⓖ 6
7 Ⓗ 7
8 Ⓘ 8
9 Ⓙ 9
Ⓚ
Ⓛ
Ⓜ
Ⓝ
Ⓞ
Ⓟ
Ⓠ
Ⓡ
Ⓢ
Ⓣ
Ⓤ
Ⓥ
Ⓦ
Ⓧ
Ⓨ
Ⓩ

7 TEST BOOK SERIAL NUMBER (Copy from front of test book.)

0 0 0 0 0 0
1 1 1 1 1 1
2 2 2 2 2 2
3 3 3 3 3 3
4 4 4 4 4 4
5 5 5 5 5 5
6 6 6 6 6 6
7 7 7 7 7 7
8 8 8 8 8 8
9 9 9 9 9 9

9 BOOK ID (Copy from back of test book.)

● Quality Assurance Mark

Chemistry *Fill in circle CE only if II is correct explanation of I.

	I	II	CE*		I	II	CE*
101	Ⓣ Ⓕ	Ⓣ Ⓕ	○	109	Ⓣ Ⓕ	Ⓣ Ⓕ	○
102	Ⓣ Ⓕ	Ⓣ Ⓕ	○	110	Ⓣ Ⓕ	Ⓣ Ⓕ	○
103	Ⓣ Ⓕ	Ⓣ Ⓕ	○	111	Ⓣ Ⓕ	Ⓣ Ⓕ	○
104	Ⓣ Ⓕ	Ⓣ Ⓕ	○	112	Ⓣ Ⓕ	Ⓣ Ⓕ	○
105	Ⓣ Ⓕ	Ⓣ Ⓕ	○	113	Ⓣ Ⓕ	Ⓣ Ⓕ	○
106	Ⓣ Ⓕ	Ⓣ Ⓕ	○	114	Ⓣ Ⓕ	Ⓣ Ⓕ	○
107	Ⓣ Ⓕ	Ⓣ Ⓕ	○	115	Ⓣ Ⓕ	Ⓣ Ⓕ	○
108	Ⓣ Ⓕ	Ⓣ Ⓕ	○				

FOR OFFICIAL USE ONLY

R/C	W/S1	FS/S2	CS/S3	WS

CERTIFICATION STATEMENT Copy the statement below and sign your name as you would an official document.

I hereby agree to the conditions set forth online at sat.collegeboard.org and in any paper registration materials given to me and certify that I am the person whose name, address and signature appear on this answer sheet.

_____

_____

_____

_____

Signature _____   Date _____

Page 2

23459 College Board 15b-10820-Text

○ Literature   ○ Mathematics Level 1   ○ German   ○ Chinese Listening   ○ Japanese Listening
○ Biology E   ○ Mathematics Level 2   ○ Italian   ○ French Listening   ○ Korean Listening
○ Biology M   ○ U.S. History   ○ Latin   ○ German Listening   ○ Spanish Listening
○ Chemistry   ○ World History   ○ Modern Hebrew
○ Physics   ○ French   ○ Spanish

Background Questions: ① ② ③ ④ ⑤ ⑥ ⑦ ⑧ ⑨

PLEASE MAKE SURE to fill in these fields completely and correctly. If they are not correct, we won't be able to score your test(s)!

1	Ⓐ Ⓑ Ⓒ Ⓓ Ⓔ	26	Ⓐ Ⓑ Ⓒ Ⓓ Ⓔ	51	Ⓐ Ⓑ Ⓒ Ⓓ Ⓔ	76	Ⓐ Ⓑ Ⓒ Ⓓ Ⓔ
2	Ⓐ Ⓑ Ⓒ Ⓓ Ⓔ	27	Ⓐ Ⓑ Ⓒ Ⓓ Ⓔ	52	Ⓐ Ⓑ Ⓒ Ⓓ Ⓔ	77	Ⓐ Ⓑ Ⓒ Ⓓ Ⓔ
3	Ⓐ Ⓑ Ⓒ Ⓓ Ⓔ	28	Ⓐ Ⓑ Ⓒ Ⓓ Ⓔ	53	Ⓐ Ⓑ Ⓒ Ⓓ Ⓔ	78	Ⓐ Ⓑ Ⓒ Ⓓ Ⓔ
4	Ⓐ Ⓑ Ⓒ Ⓓ Ⓔ	29	Ⓐ Ⓑ Ⓒ Ⓓ Ⓔ	54	Ⓐ Ⓑ Ⓒ Ⓓ Ⓔ	79	Ⓐ Ⓑ Ⓒ Ⓓ Ⓔ
5	Ⓐ Ⓑ Ⓒ Ⓓ Ⓔ	30	Ⓐ Ⓑ Ⓒ Ⓓ Ⓔ	55	Ⓐ Ⓑ Ⓒ Ⓓ Ⓔ	80	Ⓐ Ⓑ Ⓒ Ⓓ Ⓔ
6	Ⓐ Ⓑ Ⓒ Ⓓ Ⓔ	31	Ⓐ Ⓑ Ⓒ Ⓓ Ⓔ	56	Ⓐ Ⓑ Ⓒ Ⓓ Ⓔ	81	Ⓐ Ⓑ Ⓒ Ⓓ Ⓔ
7	Ⓐ Ⓑ Ⓒ Ⓓ Ⓔ	32	Ⓐ Ⓑ Ⓒ Ⓓ Ⓔ	57	Ⓐ Ⓑ Ⓒ Ⓓ Ⓔ	82	Ⓐ Ⓑ Ⓒ Ⓓ Ⓔ
8	Ⓐ Ⓑ Ⓒ Ⓓ Ⓔ	33	Ⓐ Ⓑ Ⓒ Ⓓ Ⓔ	58	Ⓐ Ⓑ Ⓒ Ⓓ Ⓔ	83	Ⓐ Ⓑ Ⓒ Ⓓ Ⓔ
9	Ⓐ Ⓑ Ⓒ Ⓓ Ⓔ	34	Ⓐ Ⓑ Ⓒ Ⓓ Ⓔ	59	Ⓐ Ⓑ Ⓒ Ⓓ Ⓔ	84	Ⓐ Ⓑ Ⓒ Ⓓ Ⓔ
10	Ⓐ Ⓑ Ⓒ Ⓓ Ⓔ	35	Ⓐ Ⓑ Ⓒ Ⓓ Ⓔ	60	Ⓐ Ⓑ Ⓒ Ⓓ Ⓔ	85	Ⓐ Ⓑ Ⓒ Ⓓ Ⓔ
11	Ⓐ Ⓑ Ⓒ Ⓓ Ⓔ	36	Ⓐ Ⓑ Ⓒ Ⓓ Ⓔ	61	Ⓐ Ⓑ Ⓒ Ⓓ Ⓔ	86	Ⓐ Ⓑ Ⓒ Ⓓ Ⓔ
12	Ⓐ Ⓑ Ⓒ Ⓓ Ⓔ	37	Ⓐ Ⓑ Ⓒ Ⓓ Ⓔ	62	Ⓐ Ⓑ Ⓒ Ⓓ Ⓔ	87	Ⓐ Ⓑ Ⓒ Ⓓ Ⓔ
13	Ⓐ Ⓑ Ⓒ Ⓓ Ⓔ	38	Ⓐ Ⓑ Ⓒ Ⓓ Ⓔ	63	Ⓐ Ⓑ Ⓒ Ⓓ Ⓔ	88	Ⓐ Ⓑ Ⓒ Ⓓ Ⓔ
14	Ⓐ Ⓑ Ⓒ Ⓓ Ⓔ	39	Ⓐ Ⓑ Ⓒ Ⓓ Ⓔ	64	Ⓐ Ⓑ Ⓒ Ⓓ Ⓔ	89	Ⓐ Ⓑ Ⓒ Ⓓ Ⓔ
15	Ⓐ Ⓑ Ⓒ Ⓓ Ⓔ	40	Ⓐ Ⓑ Ⓒ Ⓓ Ⓔ	65	Ⓐ Ⓑ Ⓒ Ⓓ Ⓔ	90	Ⓐ Ⓑ Ⓒ Ⓓ Ⓔ
16	Ⓐ Ⓑ Ⓒ Ⓓ Ⓔ	41	Ⓐ Ⓑ Ⓒ Ⓓ Ⓔ	66	Ⓐ Ⓑ Ⓒ Ⓓ Ⓔ	91	Ⓐ Ⓑ Ⓒ Ⓓ Ⓔ
17	Ⓐ Ⓑ Ⓒ Ⓓ Ⓔ	42	Ⓐ Ⓑ Ⓒ Ⓓ Ⓔ	67	Ⓐ Ⓑ Ⓒ Ⓓ Ⓔ	92	Ⓐ Ⓑ Ⓒ Ⓓ Ⓔ
18	Ⓐ Ⓑ Ⓒ Ⓓ Ⓔ	43	Ⓐ Ⓑ Ⓒ Ⓓ Ⓔ	68	Ⓐ Ⓑ Ⓒ Ⓓ Ⓔ	93	Ⓐ Ⓑ Ⓒ Ⓓ Ⓔ
19	Ⓐ Ⓑ Ⓒ Ⓓ Ⓔ	44	Ⓐ Ⓑ Ⓒ Ⓓ Ⓔ	69	Ⓐ Ⓑ Ⓒ Ⓓ Ⓔ	94	Ⓐ Ⓑ Ⓒ Ⓓ Ⓔ
20	Ⓐ Ⓑ Ⓒ Ⓓ Ⓔ	45	Ⓐ Ⓑ Ⓒ Ⓓ Ⓔ	70	Ⓐ Ⓑ Ⓒ Ⓓ Ⓔ	95	Ⓐ Ⓑ Ⓒ Ⓓ Ⓔ
21	Ⓐ Ⓑ Ⓒ Ⓓ Ⓔ	46	Ⓐ Ⓑ Ⓒ Ⓓ Ⓔ	71	Ⓐ Ⓑ Ⓒ Ⓓ Ⓔ	96	Ⓐ Ⓑ Ⓒ Ⓓ Ⓔ
22	Ⓐ Ⓑ Ⓒ Ⓓ Ⓔ	47	Ⓐ Ⓑ Ⓒ Ⓓ Ⓔ	72	Ⓐ Ⓑ Ⓒ Ⓓ Ⓔ	97	Ⓐ Ⓑ Ⓒ Ⓓ Ⓔ
23	Ⓐ Ⓑ Ⓒ Ⓓ Ⓔ	48	Ⓐ Ⓑ Ⓒ Ⓓ Ⓔ	73	Ⓐ Ⓑ Ⓒ Ⓓ Ⓔ	98	Ⓐ Ⓑ Ⓒ Ⓓ Ⓔ
24	Ⓐ Ⓑ Ⓒ Ⓓ Ⓔ	49	Ⓐ Ⓑ Ⓒ Ⓓ Ⓔ	74	Ⓐ Ⓑ Ⓒ Ⓓ Ⓔ	99	Ⓐ Ⓑ Ⓒ Ⓓ Ⓔ
25	Ⓐ Ⓑ Ⓒ Ⓓ Ⓔ	50	Ⓐ Ⓑ Ⓒ Ⓓ Ⓔ	75	Ⓐ Ⓑ Ⓒ Ⓓ Ⓔ	100	Ⓐ Ⓑ Ⓒ Ⓓ Ⓔ

Quality Assurance Mark ●

7 TEST BOOK SERIAL NUMBER
(Copy from front of test book.)

8 BOOK CODE
(Copy and grid as on back of test book.)

0 Ⓐ 0
1 Ⓑ 1
2 Ⓒ 2
3 Ⓓ 3
4 Ⓔ 4
5 Ⓕ 5
6 Ⓖ 6
7 Ⓗ 7
8 Ⓘ 8
9 Ⓙ 9
Ⓚ
Ⓛ
Ⓜ
Ⓝ
Ⓞ
Ⓟ
Ⓠ
Ⓡ
Ⓢ
Ⓣ
Ⓤ
Ⓥ
Ⓦ
Ⓧ
Ⓨ
Ⓩ

(Serial number grid: 0 0 0 0 0 0 / 1 1 1 1 1 1 / 2 2 2 2 2 2 / 3 3 3 3 3 3 / 4 4 4 4 4 4 / 5 5 5 5 5 5 / 6 6 6 6 6 6 / 7 7 7 7 7 7 / 8 8 8 8 8 8 / 9 9 9 9 9 9)

9 BOOK ID
(Copy from back of test book.)

Chemistry *Fill in circle CE only if II is correct explanation of I.

	I	II	CE*		I	II	CE*
101	Ⓣ Ⓕ	Ⓣ Ⓕ	○	109	Ⓣ Ⓕ	Ⓣ Ⓕ	○
102	Ⓣ Ⓕ	Ⓣ Ⓕ	○	110	Ⓣ Ⓕ	Ⓣ Ⓕ	○
103	Ⓣ Ⓕ	Ⓣ Ⓕ	○	111	Ⓣ Ⓕ	Ⓣ Ⓕ	○
104	Ⓣ Ⓕ	Ⓣ Ⓕ	○	112	Ⓣ Ⓕ	Ⓣ Ⓕ	○
105	Ⓣ Ⓕ	Ⓣ Ⓕ	○	113	Ⓣ Ⓕ	Ⓣ Ⓕ	○
106	Ⓣ Ⓕ	Ⓣ Ⓕ	○	114	Ⓣ Ⓕ	Ⓣ Ⓕ	○
107	Ⓣ Ⓕ	Ⓣ Ⓕ	○	115	Ⓣ Ⓕ	Ⓣ Ⓕ	○
108	Ⓣ Ⓕ	Ⓣ Ⓕ	○				

FOR OFFICIAL USE ONLY				
R/C	W/S1	FS/S2	CS/S3	WS

COMPLETE MARK ●	EXAMPLES OF INCOMPLETE MARKS Ⓐ ⊗ ⊖ Ⓒ ⊘ Ⓓ ⊜ Ⓔ	You must use a No. 2 pencil and marks must be complete. Do not use a mechanical pencil. It is very important that you fill in the entire circle darkly and completely. If you change your response, erase as completely as possible. Incomplete marks or erasures may affect your score.

- ○ Literature
- ○ Biology E
- ○ Biology M
- ○ Chemistry
- ○ Physics
- ○ Mathematics Level 1
- ○ Mathematics Level 2
- ○ U.S. History
- ○ World History
- ○ French
- ○ German
- ○ Italian
- ○ Latin
- ○ Modern Hebrew
- ○ Spanish
- ○ Chinese Listening
- ○ French Listening
- ○ German Listening
- ○ Japanese Listening
- ○ Korean Listening
- ○ Spanish Listening

Background Questions: ① ② ③ ④ ⑤ ⑥ ⑦ ⑧ ⑨

Answer grid, questions 1–100, options A B C D E

7 TEST BOOK SERIAL NUMBER (Copy from front of test book.) — columns of digits 0–9

8 BOOK CODE (Copy and grid as on back of test book.) — columns 0–9 / A–Z

9 BOOK ID (Copy from back of test book.)

Quality Assurance Mark ●

Chemistry *Fill in circle CE only if II is correct explanation of I.

	I	II	CE*		I	II	CE*
101	T F	T F	○	109	T F	T F	○
102	T F	T F	○	110	T F	T F	○
103	T F	T F	○	111	T F	T F	○
104	T F	T F	○	112	T F	T F	○
105	T F	T F	○	113	T F	T F	○
106	T F	T F	○	114	T F	T F	○
107	T F	T F	○	115	T F	T F	○
108	T F	T F	○				

FOR OFFICIAL USE ONLY				
R/C	W/S1	FS/S2	CS/S3	WS

Page 4

PLEASE DO NOT WRITE IN THIS AREA

SERIAL #

23459 College Board 15b-10820-Text

SAT Subject Tests™

1 Your Name:
(Print)

Last   First   M.I.

I agree to the conditions on the front and back of the SAT Subject Tests™ book. I also agree with the SAT Test Security and Fairness policies and understand that any violation of these policies will result in score cancellation and may result in reporting of certain violations to law enforcement.

Signature: _____   **Today's Date:** __ / __ / __
                                                           MM   DD   YY

Home Address: _____
(Print)   Number and Street   City   State/Country   Zip Code

Phone: (   ) _____   **Test Center:** _____
                              (Print)   City   State/Country

2 YOUR NAME

Last Name (First 6 Letters)   First Name (First 4 Letters)   Mid. Init.

3 DATE OF BIRTH

MONTH   DAY   YEAR

Jan, Feb, Mar, Apr, May, Jun, Jul, Aug, Sep, Oct, Nov, Dec

4 REGISTRATION NUMBER
(Copy from Admission Ticket.)

Important: Fill in items 8 and 9 exactly as shown on the back of test book.

7 TEST BOOK SERIAL NUMBER
(Copy from front of test book.)

8 BOOK CODE
(Copy and grid as on back of test book.)

0 A 0
1 B 1
2 C 2
3 D 3
4 E 4
5 F 5
6 G 6
7 H 7
8 I 8
9 J 9
K
L
M
N
O
P
Q
R
S
T
U
V
W
X
Y
Z

9 BOOK ID
(Copy from back of test book.)

PLEASE MAKE SURE to fill in these fields completely and correctly. If they are not correct, we won't be able to score your test(s)!

5 ZIP CODE

6 TEST CENTER
(Supplied by Test Center Supervisor.)

FOR OFFICIAL USE ONLY
0 1 2 3 4 5 6
0 1 2 3 4 5 6
0 1 2 3 4 5 6

103648-77191 • NS1114C1085 • Printed in U.S.A.

194415-001   1 2 3 4 5 A B C D E   Printed in the USA   ISD11312

783175

PLEASE DO NOT WRITE IN THIS AREA   **SERIAL #**

23459 College Board 15b-10820-Text

| COMPLETE MARK ● | EXAMPLES OF INCOMPLETE MARKS ⓐ ⊗ ⊖ ⓒ ⊝ ⊘ ⊘ ⓑ | You must use a No. 2 pencil and marks must be complete. Do not use a mechanical pencil. It is very important that you fill in the entire circle darkly and completely. If you change your response, erase as completely as possible. Incomplete marks or erasures may affect your score. |

○ Literature
○ Biology E
○ Biology M
○ Chemistry
○ Physics

○ Mathematics Level 1
○ Mathematics Level 2
○ U.S. History
○ World History
○ French

○ German
○ Italian
○ Latin
○ Modern Hebrew
○ Spanish

○ Chinese Listening
○ French Listening
○ German Listening

○ Japanese Listening
○ Korean Listening
○ Spanish Listening

Background Questions: ① ② ③ ④ ⑤ ⑥ ⑦ ⑧ ⑨

1 Ⓐ Ⓑ Ⓒ Ⓓ Ⓔ   26 Ⓐ Ⓑ Ⓒ Ⓓ Ⓔ   51 Ⓐ Ⓑ Ⓒ Ⓓ Ⓔ   76 Ⓐ Ⓑ Ⓒ Ⓓ Ⓔ
2 Ⓐ Ⓑ Ⓒ Ⓓ Ⓔ   27 Ⓐ Ⓑ Ⓒ Ⓓ Ⓔ   52 Ⓐ Ⓑ Ⓒ Ⓓ Ⓔ   77 Ⓐ Ⓑ Ⓒ Ⓓ Ⓔ
3 Ⓐ Ⓑ Ⓒ Ⓓ Ⓔ   28 Ⓐ Ⓑ Ⓒ Ⓓ Ⓔ   53 Ⓐ Ⓑ Ⓒ Ⓓ Ⓔ   78 Ⓐ Ⓑ Ⓒ Ⓓ Ⓔ
4 Ⓐ Ⓑ Ⓒ Ⓓ Ⓔ   29 Ⓐ Ⓑ Ⓒ Ⓓ Ⓔ   54 Ⓐ Ⓑ Ⓒ Ⓓ Ⓔ   79 Ⓐ Ⓑ Ⓒ Ⓓ Ⓔ
5 Ⓐ Ⓑ Ⓒ Ⓓ Ⓔ   30 Ⓐ Ⓑ Ⓒ Ⓓ Ⓔ   55 Ⓐ Ⓑ Ⓒ Ⓓ Ⓔ   80 Ⓐ Ⓑ Ⓒ Ⓓ Ⓔ
6 Ⓐ Ⓑ Ⓒ Ⓓ Ⓔ   31 Ⓐ Ⓑ Ⓒ Ⓓ Ⓔ   56 Ⓐ Ⓑ Ⓒ Ⓓ Ⓔ   81 Ⓐ Ⓑ Ⓒ Ⓓ Ⓔ
7 Ⓐ Ⓑ Ⓒ Ⓓ Ⓔ   32 Ⓐ Ⓑ Ⓒ Ⓓ Ⓔ   57 Ⓐ Ⓑ Ⓒ Ⓓ Ⓔ   82 Ⓐ Ⓑ Ⓒ Ⓓ Ⓔ
8 Ⓐ Ⓑ Ⓒ Ⓓ Ⓔ   33 Ⓐ Ⓑ Ⓒ Ⓓ Ⓔ   58 Ⓐ Ⓑ Ⓒ Ⓓ Ⓔ   83 Ⓐ Ⓑ Ⓒ Ⓓ Ⓔ
9 Ⓐ Ⓑ Ⓒ Ⓓ Ⓔ   34 Ⓐ Ⓑ Ⓒ Ⓓ Ⓔ   59 Ⓐ Ⓑ Ⓒ Ⓓ Ⓔ   84 Ⓐ Ⓑ Ⓒ Ⓓ Ⓔ
10 Ⓐ Ⓑ Ⓒ Ⓓ Ⓔ   35 Ⓐ Ⓑ Ⓒ Ⓓ Ⓔ   60 Ⓐ Ⓑ Ⓒ Ⓓ Ⓔ   85 Ⓐ Ⓑ Ⓒ Ⓓ Ⓔ
11 Ⓐ Ⓑ Ⓒ Ⓓ Ⓔ   36 Ⓐ Ⓑ Ⓒ Ⓓ Ⓔ   61 Ⓐ Ⓑ Ⓒ Ⓓ Ⓔ   86 Ⓐ Ⓑ Ⓒ Ⓓ Ⓔ
12 Ⓐ Ⓑ Ⓒ Ⓓ Ⓔ   37 Ⓐ Ⓑ Ⓒ Ⓓ Ⓔ   62 Ⓐ Ⓑ Ⓒ Ⓓ Ⓔ   87 Ⓐ Ⓑ Ⓒ Ⓓ Ⓔ
13 Ⓐ Ⓑ Ⓒ Ⓓ Ⓔ   38 Ⓐ Ⓑ Ⓒ Ⓓ Ⓔ   63 Ⓐ Ⓑ Ⓒ Ⓓ Ⓔ   88 Ⓐ Ⓑ Ⓒ Ⓓ Ⓔ
14 Ⓐ Ⓑ Ⓒ Ⓓ Ⓔ   39 Ⓐ Ⓑ Ⓒ Ⓓ Ⓔ   64 Ⓐ Ⓑ Ⓒ Ⓓ Ⓔ   89 Ⓐ Ⓑ Ⓒ Ⓓ Ⓔ
15 Ⓐ Ⓑ Ⓒ Ⓓ Ⓔ   40 Ⓐ Ⓑ Ⓒ Ⓓ Ⓔ   65 Ⓐ Ⓑ Ⓒ Ⓓ Ⓔ   90 Ⓐ Ⓑ Ⓒ Ⓓ Ⓔ
16 Ⓐ Ⓑ Ⓒ Ⓓ Ⓔ   41 Ⓐ Ⓑ Ⓒ Ⓓ Ⓔ   66 Ⓐ Ⓑ Ⓒ Ⓓ Ⓔ   91 Ⓐ Ⓑ Ⓒ Ⓓ Ⓔ
17 Ⓐ Ⓑ Ⓒ Ⓓ Ⓔ   42 Ⓐ Ⓑ Ⓒ Ⓓ Ⓔ   67 Ⓐ Ⓑ Ⓒ Ⓓ Ⓔ   92 Ⓐ Ⓑ Ⓒ Ⓓ Ⓔ
18 Ⓐ Ⓑ Ⓒ Ⓓ Ⓔ   43 Ⓐ Ⓑ Ⓒ Ⓓ Ⓔ   68 Ⓐ Ⓑ Ⓒ Ⓓ Ⓔ   93 Ⓐ Ⓑ Ⓒ Ⓓ Ⓔ
19 Ⓐ Ⓑ Ⓒ Ⓓ Ⓔ   44 Ⓐ Ⓑ Ⓒ Ⓓ Ⓔ   69 Ⓐ Ⓑ Ⓒ Ⓓ Ⓔ   94 Ⓐ Ⓑ Ⓒ Ⓓ Ⓔ
20 Ⓐ Ⓑ Ⓒ Ⓓ Ⓔ   45 Ⓐ Ⓑ Ⓒ Ⓓ Ⓔ   70 Ⓐ Ⓑ Ⓒ Ⓓ Ⓔ   95 Ⓐ Ⓑ Ⓒ Ⓓ Ⓔ
21 Ⓐ Ⓑ Ⓒ Ⓓ Ⓔ   46 Ⓐ Ⓑ Ⓒ Ⓓ Ⓔ   71 Ⓐ Ⓑ Ⓒ Ⓓ Ⓔ   96 Ⓐ Ⓑ Ⓒ Ⓓ Ⓔ
22 Ⓐ Ⓑ Ⓒ Ⓓ Ⓔ   47 Ⓐ Ⓑ Ⓒ Ⓓ Ⓔ   72 Ⓐ Ⓑ Ⓒ Ⓓ Ⓔ   97 Ⓐ Ⓑ Ⓒ Ⓓ Ⓔ
23 Ⓐ Ⓑ Ⓒ Ⓓ Ⓔ   48 Ⓐ Ⓑ Ⓒ Ⓓ Ⓔ   73 Ⓐ Ⓑ Ⓒ Ⓓ Ⓔ   98 Ⓐ Ⓑ Ⓒ Ⓓ Ⓔ
24 Ⓐ Ⓑ Ⓒ Ⓓ Ⓔ   49 Ⓐ Ⓑ Ⓒ Ⓓ Ⓔ   74 Ⓐ Ⓑ Ⓒ Ⓓ Ⓔ   99 Ⓐ Ⓑ Ⓒ Ⓓ Ⓔ
25 Ⓐ Ⓑ Ⓒ Ⓓ Ⓔ   50 Ⓐ Ⓑ Ⓒ Ⓓ Ⓔ   75 Ⓐ Ⓑ Ⓒ Ⓓ Ⓔ   100 Ⓐ Ⓑ Ⓒ Ⓓ Ⓔ

PLEASE MAKE SURE to fill in these fields completely and correctly. If they are not correct, we won't be able to score your test(s)!

7 TEST BOOK SERIAL NUMBER (Copy from front of test book.)

8 BOOK CODE (Copy and grid as on back of test book.)

9 BOOK ID (Copy from back of test book.)

Quality Assurance Mark ●

Chemistry *Fill in circle CE only if II is correct explanation of I.

	I	II	CE*		I	II	CE*
101	T F	T F	○	109	T F	T F	○
102	T F	T F	○	110	T F	T F	○
103	T F	T F	○	111	T F	T F	○
104	T F	T F	○	112	T F	T F	○
105	T F	T F	○	113	T F	T F	○
106	T F	T F	○	114	T F	T F	○
107	T F	T F	○	115	T F	T F	○
108	T F	T F	○				

FOR OFFICIAL USE ONLY				
R/C	W/S1	FS/S2	CS/S3	WS

CERTIFICATION STATEMENT Copy the statement below and sign your name as you would an official document.

I hereby agree to the conditions set forth online at sat.collegeboard.org and in any paper registration materials given to me and certify that I am the person whose name, address and signature appear on this answer sheet.

_____

_____

_____

Signature _____   Date _____

Page 2

23459 College Board 15b-10820-Text

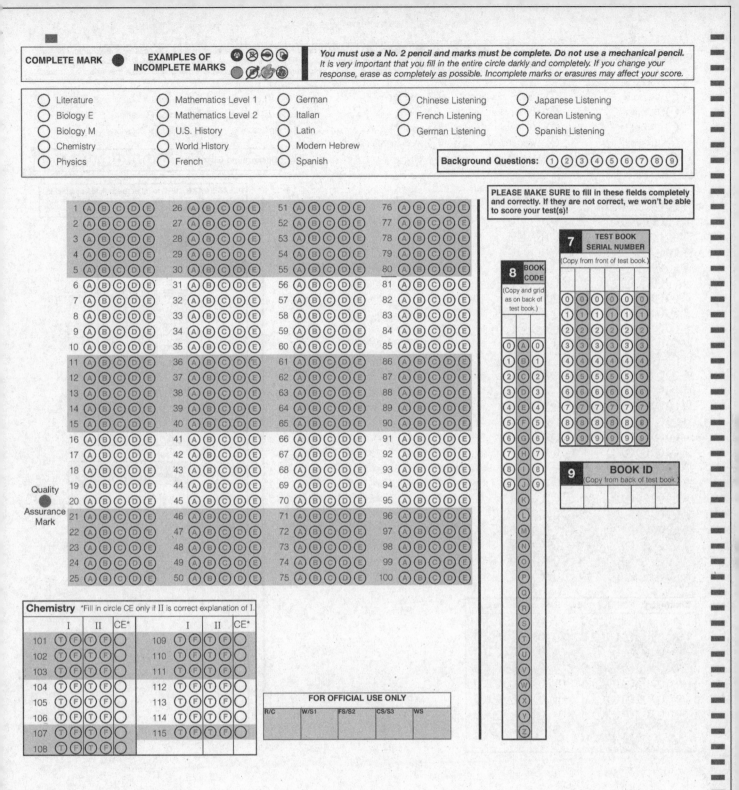

23459 College Board 15b-10820-Text

○ Literature
○ Biology E
○ Biology M
○ Chemistry
○ Physics

○ Mathematics Level 1
○ Mathematics Level 2
○ U.S. History
○ World History
○ French

○ German
○ Italian
○ Latin
○ Modern Hebrew
○ Spanish

○ Chinese Listening
○ French Listening
○ German Listening

○ Japanese Listening
○ Korean Listening
○ Spanish Listening

Background Questions: ① ② ③ ④ ⑤ ⑥ ⑦ ⑧ ⑨

PLEASE MAKE SURE to fill in these fields completely and correctly. If they are not correct, we won't be able to score your test(s)!

1–100: A B C D E (multiple choice answer grid, questions 1 through 100)

8 BOOK CODE (Copy and grid as on back of test book.)
Columns: 0–9 digits, A–Z letters

7 TEST BOOK SERIAL NUMBER (Copy from front of test book.)
0–9 digit columns

9 BOOK ID (Copy from back of test book.)

Quality Assurance Mark ●

Chemistry *Fill in circle CE only if II is correct explanation of I.

	I	II	CE*		I	II	CE*
101	T F	T F	○	109	T F	T F	○
102	T F	T F	○	110	T F	T F	○
103	T F	T F	○	111	T F	T F	○
104	T F	T F	○	112	T F	T F	○
105	T F	T F	○	113	T F	T F	○
106	T F	T F	○	114	T F	T F	○
107	T F	T F	○	115	T F	T F	○
108	T F	T F	○				

FOR OFFICIAL USE ONLY				
R/C	W/S1	FS/S2	CS/S3	WS

Page 4

PLEASE DO NOT WRITE IN THIS AREA
○○○○○○○○○○○○○○○○○○○○○○○○○○○○

SERIAL #

23459 College Board 15b-10820-Text

Show up ready on test day.

There are over 50 videos to watch covering lots of physics topics. These lessons are great refreshers to help you get ready for the Physics Subject Test. And, you can also access video lesson playlists for Biology and Chemistry.

Disclaimer: Playlists were created based on videos available on Khan Academy. The contents are subject to change in the future.

Want **free** online lessons from Khan Academy*?

Check out **satsubjecttests.org/physics**.